We Are All Apocalyptic Now:

On the Responsibilities of Teaching, Preaching, Reporting, Writing, and Speaking Out

Robert Jensen

We Are All Apocalyptic Now: On the Responsibilities of Teaching, Preaching, Reporting, Writing, and Speaking Out

First Edition
© 2013 by Robert William Jensen

Published by Robert Jensen in conjunction with the MonkeyWrench Books collective. Cover and design by David Steadman.
Fonts: Adobe Caslon Pro, Benton Sans and Suomi Hand
robertwilliamjensen@gmail.com

In loving memory of Jim Koplin (1933-2012)

Introduction: Get Apocalyptic   4

Chapter 1: What is an Apocalypse?   7

Chapter 2: What is an Intellectual?   10

Chapter 3: The Condition of the World   14

Chapter 4: The Systems of the World   22

Chapter 5: Reasonable Responses   36

Chapter 6: Intellectuals' Failures   42

Chapter 7: The Myth of the Neutral Intellectual   51

Chapter 8: Journalism: Royal, Prophetic, Apocalyptic   56

Conclusion: Future Hope?   66

Introduction:
Get Apocalyptic

Responsible intellectuals need to think apocalyptically.

That may seem counterintuitive—aren't responsible intellectuals supposed to be careful and cautious? So, let's start with a role model: British astronomer Martin Rees, who in recent years has been suggesting that human civilization is on increasingly shaky ground. That's Sir Martin John Rees, a Fellow of Trinity College and Emeritus Professor of Cosmology and Astrophysics at the University of Cambridge, who holds the honorary title of Astronomer Royal and was president of the Royal Society from 2005–2010. Sir Martin has all the credentials of a very responsible intellectual.

When Rees' book outlining the ways humans may self-destruct in the near future was released in the UK in 2003, it was titled *Our Final Century: Will the Human Race Survive the Twenty-first Century?* The following year it was published in the United States as *Our Final Hour: A Scientist's Warning: How Terror, Error, and Environmental Disaster Threaten Humankind's Future in This Century—On Earth and Beyond.*[1]

Well, which is it—a century or an hour? If we want to keep track of humans' shaky future, do we need a calendar or a stopwatch? There's no way to know for sure, of course, and Rees' book offers no predictions; it's a measured, sober analysis of some of the serious risks we face, not an eschatological rant. The change in the title was no doubt the decision of people in marketing, not scientists. But whatever the exact timeline of the threat, reasonable people should be paying attention.

One of the jobs of intellectuals is to identify the issues to which we should be paying attention, even when—especially when—people would prefer to ignore problems. Intellectuals today should be apocalyptic, focusing attention—and a lot of our attention—on the hard-to-face realities of an unjust and unsustainable world. Today, the distribution of wealth and power around the world fails to meet even minimal moral standards. Looking ahead, our assault on the ecosphere makes it unlikely that the planet will be able to support large-scale human civilization as we know it without significant changes in the way we arrange our lives.

In the face of increasing inequality within the human family that

---

1   Martin Rees, *Our Final Hour: A Scientist's Warning: How Terror, Error, and Environmental Disaster Threaten Humankind's Future in This Century—On Earth and Beyond* (New York: Basic Books, 2004).

is playing out in an increasingly fragile natural world, we are all—or should be—apocalyptic now, and intellectuals need to step up and do their part.

Defending that claim has to start with definitions, because most intellectuals associate apocalypticism with fantastical talk of rapture and tribulation, end-time cults, or science fiction; and most ordinary people tend not to like and/or trust intellectuals. After offering a calm apocalypticism and a common-sense approach to intellectual life, this manifesto will address these questions: What is the condition of the world? What systems have brought us to that state of affairs? How might reasonable people, including intellectuals, respond to these realities? Why are so few intellectuals being reasonable? From there, I will explain why the alleged neutrality behind which so many intellectuals hide is a myth, and then use journalism as a case study to illuminate the possibilities and limitations within intellectual institutions, examining three possible journalistic orientations: royal, prophetic, and apocalyptic. The essay will conclude with reflections on what hopes there might be for a future.

Chapter 1: What is an Apocalypse?

Speaking apocalyptically need not leave us stuck in a corner with the folks predicting lakes of fire, rivers of blood, or bodies lifted up to the heavens. Many people assume apocalypticism leads to claims that the world is about to end, usually accompanied by a belief in the ability of the chosen to transcend that fate completely or at least successfully weather a transition to a new world. Indeed, many apocalyptic visions—both religious and secular—imagine the replacement of a corrupt society by one structured on principles that will redeem humanity, or at least redeem those who sign onto the principles. But this need not be our only understanding of the term.

If we are not limited to fear-driven fantasies and self-indulgent claims of special selection, we can invoke a different notion of apocalypse, crafted not to justify theological solipsism, self-righteousness, and separation from others, but to deepen our sense of humility and remind us of the need for greater collaboration across differences. Thinking apocalyptically can help us confront honestly the crises of our time and strategize constructively about possible responses. It's simply about struggling to understand—to the best of our ability, without succumbing to magical thinking—the conditions within the human family and the state of the ecosphere, and not turning away from the difficult realities we face.

Most discussions of revelation and apocalypse in contemporary America focus on the Book of Revelation, also known as The Apocalypse of John, the final book of the Christian New Testament. The two terms are synonymous in their original meaning; "revelation" from Latin and "apocalypse" from Greek both mean a lifting of the veil, a disclosure of something hidden from most people, a coming to clarity. Many scholars interpret the Book of Revelation not as a set of predictions about the future but as a critique of the oppression of the Roman Empire.[2] To speak apocalyptically, in that context, is first and foremost about deepening our understanding of the world, seeing through the illusions that people in power create to keep us trapped in systems they control. In the propaganda-saturated world in which we live in the contemporary United States, coming to that kind of clarity about the nature of the empires of our day is always a

---

2   For varying readings, see David L. Barr, *Tales of the End: A Narrative Commentary on the Book of Revelation* (Santa Rosa, CA: Polebridge Press, 1998); Wes Howard-Brook, *"Come Out My People!": God's Call Out of Empire in the Bible and Beyond* (Maryknoll, NY: Orbis Books, 2010); and Elaine Pagels, *Revelations: Visions, Prophecy, and Politics in the Book of Revelation* (New York: Viking, 2012).

struggle, and that notion of revelation is more crucial than ever.

Thinking apocalyptically, coming to this clarity, will force us to confront crises that concentrated wealth and power create. It is not crazy to look at the state of the world—economically, politically, culturally, and ecologically—and conclude that there are rocky times ahead (more specifics on that later). Unfortunately, in popular culture and mainstream political discourse the term "apocalypse" has become synonymous with a reactionary theology which turns that particular book of the Bible into the handbook for a death cult's predictions of horrors to come and fantasies about a magical deliverance.

Instead of predicting the rapture to come, apocalyptic vision can help us understand social and ecological ruptures in the here and now. Responsible apocalyptic thinking, such as Rees', does not assume a set script already written by a divine hand or offer pseudo-scientific predictions, but rather reminds us of the importance of dealing honestly with reality even when it's frightening, and holding onto our humanity, which is even more important when we're frightened. Given the severity of the human assault on the ecosphere, compounded by the suffering and strife within the human family, honest apocalyptic thinking that is firmly grounded in a systematic evaluation of the state of the world is not only sensible but a moral obligation.

Because people typically associate "apocalypse" with predictions about the end of the existing world and a perfect new world beyond, let me repeat: Rather than thinking of revelation as divine delivery of a clear message about some fantastic future above, we can engage in an ongoing process of revelation that results from an honest struggle to understand, a process that requires a lot of effort. Things are bad, systems are failing, and the status quo won't last forever. Thinking apocalyptically in this fashion demands of us considerable courage and commitment. This process will not produce definitive answers but rather help us identify new directions.

Chapter 2: What is an Intellectual?

Ordinary people often express a lack of respect for and/or distrust of intellectuals, whom they see as elitist snobs flashing academic credentials as proof of superiority. That assessment is in many cases on target; intellectuals—especially university professors—have done a lot to earn this resentment[3] and should be critiqued. But we shouldn't minimize the importance of real intellectual effort—the task of understanding how the world works and communicating that understanding to others—just because we are annoyed with the arrogance and self-indulgence of a privileged group.

First, the term "intellectual work" is not just a synonym for "thinking." Every day everyone thinks about things. Intellectual work suggests a systematic effort to (1) collect relevant information and (2) analyze that information to discern patterns that help us deepen our understanding of how the world works, (3) to help us make judgments about how we want to shape the world. The key is "systematic effort," which requires intention and discipline. Defined that way, it's clear that lots of different kinds of people do this kind of intellectual work—not just professors, but students, organizers, political activists, journalists, and writers and researchers of various kinds. They engage in that systematic effort in search of the answers to questions about the natural world, technology, human behavior, societies. Some focus on fairly small questions while others look more broadly.[4]

Societies subsidize intellectual work, allowing certain people the freedom to engage in those systematic efforts while others do the work of producing food, building shelter, providing services. This arrangement comes with some built-in tensions, since most intellectuals are subsidized by the institutions of the dominant culture. The people who run those institutions generally expect a return on the investment, which argues for putting restrictions on the work of those subsidized intellectuals. At the same time, intellectual work requires creative and critical thinking, which argues for letting intellectuals operate with minimal control. These institutions prefer that research, writing, and teaching support the existing power system, and most intellectuals conform to that implicit expectation—either

3   For a discussion of how the intelligence of workers is denigrated, see Mike Rose, *The Mind at Work: Valuing the Intelligence of the American Worker* (New York: Penguin, 2005).
4   For a more extensive discussion, see Robert Jensen, *Arguing for Our Lives* (San Francisco: City Lights, 2013).

because they honestly believe in the system of power or because they want to avoid trouble.[5] But tensions arise when intellectuals follow paths that lead them to challenge the pre-ordained conclusions that the powerful prefer.

This creates an obvious problem for anyone attempting to be responsibly apocalyptic: The institutions that most often subsidize intellectuals (universities, think tanks, government, corporations) are the key agents of the social systems that produce inequality and threaten the stability of human life on the planet. The more that these subsidized intellectuals not only identify the dangerous patterns but highlight the pathological systems out of which the patterns emerge, the greater the tension with whoever is paying the bills.

Today, few intellectuals practice this responsible apocalypticism. As long as most intellectuals serve these systems without raising these difficult issues, it's easy for the institutions to accommodate the relatively small number of critics, who at the moment have no demonstrable effect on the trajectory of society. If more intellectuals challenged the systems and institutions, growing to the point where collectively they could begin to influence more people and possibly change that trajectory, that tension would increase dramatically. As is often the case, one's success can be measured by the degree to which power takes notice and takes action against challenges. Today, power doesn't have to worry.

This doesn't doom resistance politics, since subsidized intellectuals are not the only people who can understand how the world works, nor are intellectuals the natural leaders of progressive or radical movements. Some kinds of intellectual work require specialized training, which means some people will play special roles in some endeavors. In a technologically advanced society, obviously no one person can acquire the knowledge of every process and technology, and so we have to rely on specialists' expertise in some arenas. But especially on matters of social, political, and economic policy, everyone is capable of developing the intellectual abilities needed to contribute to the cultural conversation about our goals. We don't need to be specialists to develop viewpoints that we can defend in

---

5   For a foundational discussion of this in the context of the United States, see Noam Chomsky, "The Responsibility of Intellectuals," *New York Review of Books*, February 23, 1967. http://www.nybooks.com/articles/archives/1967/feb/23/a-special-supplement-the-responsibility-of-intelle/

dialogue with others. In a healthy democratic system, experts serve the greater good rather than dictate it.

A sensible way to begin a discussion of that greater good is to focus on the current conditions within the human family and on the state of the larger living world.

Chapter 3:
The Condition of
the World

How are wealth and well-being distributed among people, and is that distribution consistent with our basic moral and theological principles? How are the planet's ecosystems faring, and are the ways we are currently living in the world consistent with a stable long-term human presence? If we look at the data regarding these crucial categories of social justice and ecological sustainability, the news is disturbing.

Social Justice

About the only good news on the social justice front is that the number of people in "extreme poverty"—defined as living on less than $1.25 a day, the edge of survival—has been dropping for the past two decades.[6] That's an improvement, of sorts, but we might want to postpone a celebration. Even with that "good" news, a third of the people on the planet to live on less than $2 per day, while half live on less than $2.50 a day.[7] More than 3 billion people survive—struggling for food, shelter, clothing, education, medical care—on less than what those in the privileged sectors of the developed world might spend on a fancy cup of coffee one morning.

Inequality is a permanent feature of capitalism, and the gap between rich and poor is growing. In the United States, the top 20 percent of people own 85 percent of the country's wealth, which means the bottom 80 percent of the population share the remaining 15 percent of the wealth.[8] In recent years, the top 1 percent are doing even better, capturing almost one quarter of the nation's income and controlling 40 percent of the wealth, compared with 12 percent and 33 percent, respectively, 25 years ago.[9]

This inequality clearly is a threat to meaningfully democratic politics (more on that later) but it also undermines capitalism's own claims to rationality and efficiency by exacerbating volatility and crises, reducing productivity, and slowing growth. Inequality that leaves much of a society's population to languish in inadequate

---

6   World Bank, "Extreme poverty rates continue to fall," June 2, 2010. http://data.worldbank.org/news/extreme-poverty-rates-continue-to-fall

7   World Bank, "World Development Report 2008," October 2007. www.worldbank.org/wdr2008

8   G. William Domhoff, "Wealth, Income, and Power," July 2010. http://sociology.ucsc.edu/whorulesamerica/power/wealth.html

9   Joseph E. Stiglitz, "Of the 1%, by the 1%, for the 1%," *Vanity Fair*, May 2011. http://www.vanityfair.com/society/features/2011/05/top-one-percent-201105

schools and communities is not productive—the most valuable asset, people, is being "used" irrationally and inefficiently.[10]

There are lots of ways to slice and dice income and wealth statistics to highlight or obscure this inequality,[11] but these days the defenders of the wealthy don't deny the growing disparities and instead focus on making moral and practical arguments: Rich people deserve their riches because of their superior abilities, and besides we had better be nice to them if we don't want to spook them into hoarding their wealth even more.[12]

In the United States, this class divide is also racialized, which is hardly surprising in a nation that has never transcended the white-supremacist ideology on which it was founded. The reports from United for a Fair Economy, which produces some of the best ongoing studies of this racialized inequality, indicates that disparities in income will continue to perpetuate poverty in communities of color unless changes are made, and that increasing wealth inequality overall entrenches the racial economic divide. The consequences of this racialized disparity are most glaringly evident in the makeup of the U.S. prison population; blacks are six times more likely to be in prison than whites, and people of color make up over 65 percent of the prison population. Largely as a result of a so-called "war on drugs," 68 percent of black men born since the mid-1970s have prison records.[13] The racialized implementation of drug laws has created a "new Jim Crow"[14] that a leading analyst calls "a racial caste system [that] is alive and well in America."[15]

Highlighting these enduring racial patterns does not minimize the hard-fought victories of the movement for voting and civil

---

10 Joseph E. Stiglitz, *The Price of Inequality* (New York: W.W. Norton, 2012).

11 For a sensible review, see "Scholarship on Inequality: Research Review," Journalist's Resource, August 2012. http://journalistsresource.org/studies/government/politics/income-inequality-research-roundup-storify-presentation-data-findings/

12 For example, Adam Davidson, "The Purpose of Spectacular Wealth, According to a Spectacularly Wealthy Guy," *New York Times*, May 1, 2012. http://www.nytimes.com/2012/05/06/magazine/romneys-former-bain-partner-makes-a-case-for-inequality.html?pagewanted=all The "spectacularly wealthy guy" is Edward Conard, *Unintended Consequences: Why Everything You've Been Told about the Economy Is Wrong* (New York: Penguin/Portfolio, 2012).

13 United for a Fair Economy, "State of the Dream 2012: The Emerging Majority," January 12, 2012. http://faireconomy.org/sites/default/files/State_of_the_Dream_2012.pdf

14 Michelle Alexander, *The New Jim Crow: Mass Incarceration in the Age of Colorblindness* (New York: New Press, 2010).

15 Mark Karlin, "Michelle Alexander on the Irrational Race Bias of the Criminal Justice and Prison Systems," *Truthout*, August 1, 2012. http://truth-out.org/opinion/item/10629-truthout-interviews-michelle-alexander-on-the-irrational-race-bias-of-the-criminal-justice-and-prison-systems

rights for non-white people, but makes it clear what remains to be accomplished. Similarly, feminist campaigns have won greater gender justice, but the United States remains a deeply patriarchal society, and improvements in some areas (greater access to education and jobs from which women had been excluded, for example) do nothing to resolve other deeply entrenched problems (women make up a disproportionate share of the poor, for example). One measure of the status of a class of people is the routine abuse perpetrated upon them, and the data on men's violence against women is clear: We live in a culture in which men are trained to see themselves as naturally dominant and women as naturally passive, in which women are objectified and women's sexuality is commodified, in which men eroticize women's subordinate status. The predictable result is a world in which violence, sexualized violence, sexual violence, and violence-by-sex is so common that it must be considered to be normal, that is, an expression of the sexual norms of the culture, not violations of the norms.

Studies over the years have suggested varying rape rates. For many years, anti-rape activists quoted the statistic that one in three girls is sexually abused in the United States and that 38 percent of the women reported sexual abuse before age 18.[16] A recent review of the data by well-respected researchers concluded that in the United States, at least one of every six women has been raped at some time in her life, a figure that is now widely accepted.[17] In addition to those acts legally defined as rape, women routinely experience various levels of sexual intrusion—sexual taunting on the streets, sexual harassment in schools and workplaces, coercive sexual pressure in dating, sexual assault, and violence with a sexual theme. Given the intense societal pressure on women and children not to talk about their experiences, we are not likely to ever know exactly how much sexual violence and abuse there is in this culture. But we do know that the number is so high that we cannot ignore an ugly reality: We live in a woman-hating world. No society would let happen what happens to women if at some level the people with power and

16 Diana E.H. Russell, *Sexual Exploitation: Rape, Child Sexual Abuse, and Workplace Harassment* (Beverly Hills: Sage, 1984), pp. 285–286.
17 Patricia Tjaden and Nancy Thoennes, "Extent, Nature, and Consequences of Rape Victimization: Findings from the National Violence against Women Survey," U.S. Department of Justice Office of Justice Programs, National Institute of Justice (2006). http://www.ncjrs.gov/pdffiles1/nij/210346.pdf

privilege did not have contempt for them.

The interlocking nature of injustice—the intersection of class, race, and gender—is clear. A 2005 United Nations report, aptly titled "The Inequality Predicament," stressed:

> Ignoring inequality in the pursuit of development is peril-
> ous. Focusing exclusively on economic growth and income
> generation as a development strategy is ineffective, as it
> leads to the accumulation of wealth by a few and deepens
> the poverty of many; such an approach does not acknowl-
> edge the intergenerational transmission of poverty.[18]

Ecological Sustainability

Ignoring ecological collapse in the pursuit of economic growth is equally perilous. There is a growing realization that we have dis-rupted planetary forces in ways we cannot control and do not fully understand. If we remain on our current trajectory there likely will come a point—not in some future millennium but possibly in this century—when the ecosphere cannot sustain human life as we know it. We cannot predict the specific times and places where dramatic breakdowns will occur, but we can know that the living system on which we depend is breaking down. When people ask James Howard Kunstler about the time frame for the "long emer-gency" (his phrase for our moment in history), he tells them that "we've entered the zone."[19] As Bill McKibben puts it, "The world hasn't ended, but the world as we know it has—even if we don't quite know it yet."[20]

Look at any crucial measure of the health of the ecosphere in which we live—groundwater depletion, topsoil loss, chemical con-tamination, increased toxicity in our own bodies, the number and size of "dead zones" in the oceans, accelerating extinction of species and reduction of bio-diversity—and ask a simple question: Where we are heading? Remember also that we live in an oil-based world that is

---

18 United Nations, "Report on the World Social Situation 2005: The Inequality Predicament." http://www.un.org/esa/socdev/rwss/media%2005/
19 James Howard Kunstler, *Too Much Magic: Wishful Thinking, Technology, and the Fate of the Nation* (New York: Atlantic Monthly Press, 2012), p. 2.
20 Bill McKibben, *Eaarth: Making Life on a Tough New Planet* (New York: Times Books/Henry Holt, 2010), p. 2.

rapidly depleting the cheap and easily accessible oil,[21] which means we face a huge reconfiguration of the infrastructure that undergirds our lives.[22] Meanwhile, the desperation to avoid that reconfiguration has brought us to the era of "extreme energy" using even more dangerous and destructive technologies (hydrofracturing, deep-water drilling, mountain-top removal, tar sands extraction).[23] And, of course, there is the undeniable trajectory of climate disruption.[24]

Scientists these days are talking about tipping points[25] and planetary boundaries,[26] about how human activity is pushing the planet beyond its limits. Paleoecologist Anthony Barnosky of the University of California-Berkeley and 21 colleagues warn that humans likely are forcing a planetary-scale critical transition "with the potential to transform Earth rapidly and irreversibly into a state unknown in human experience."[27] That means that "the biological resources we take for granted at present may be subject to rapid and unpredictable transformations within a few human generations."

That means that we're in trouble. The authors conclude with a simple set of recommendations:

> [A]verting a planetary-scale critical transition demands global cooperation to stem current global-scale anthropogenic forcings. This will require reducing world population growth and per-capita resource use; rapidly increasing the proportion of the world's energy budget that is supplied by sources other than fossil fuels while also becoming more

---

21 One leading experts sums up this "inescapable conclusion": "[T]he major oil finds of the postwar era—those mammoth discoveries whose prolific output sustained rising global energy needs for nearly half a century—are no longer capable of satisfying the world's requirements." Michael T. Klare, *The Race for What's Left: The Global Scramble for the World's Last Resources* (New York: Metropolitan, 2012), p. 31.

22 For an accessible review of the data and a blunt evaluation of options, see James Howard Kunstler, *The Long Emergency: Surviving the End of Oil, Climate Change, and Other Converging Catastrophes of the Twenty-First Century* (New York: Grove, 2006).

23 Naomi Klein, "Addicted to Risk," TED, December 2010. http://www.ted.com/talks/naomi_klein_addicted_to_risk.html

24 Naomi Klein, "Capitalism vs. the Climate," *The Nation*, November 28, 2011. http://www.the-nation.com/article/164497/capitalism-vs-climate/; "Naomi Klein Warns Global Warming Could Be Exploited by Capitalism and Militarism," Democracy Now! March 9, 2011. http://www.democracynow.org/2011/3/9/my_fear_is_that_climate_change

25 See the June 7, 2012, issue of *Nature*.
http://www.nature.com/nature/journal/v486/n7401/index.html

26 See the September 23, 2009, issue of *Nature*.
http://www.nature.com/news/specials/planetaryboundaries/index.html

27 Anthony Barnosky, et al, "Approaching a state shift in Earth's biosphere," *Nature*, June 7, 2012. http://www.nature.com/nature/journal/v486/n7401/full/nature11018.html

efficient in using fossil fuels when they provide the only option; increasing the efficiency of existing means of food production and distribution instead of converting new areas or relying on wild species to feed people; and enhancing efforts to manage as reservoirs of biodiversity and ecosystem services, both in the terrestrial and marine realms, the parts of Earth's surface that are not already dominated by humans.

McKibben, the first popular writer to alert the world to the threat of climate change, argues that humans have so dramatically changed the planet's ecosystems that we should rename the Earth, call it Eaarth:

> The planet on which our civilization evolved no longer exists. The stability that produced that civilization has vanished; epic changes have begun. We may, with commitment and luck, yet be able to maintain a planet that will sustain some kind of civilization, but it won't be the same planet, and hence it won't be the same civilization. The earth that we knew—the only earth that we ever knew—is gone.[28]

If McKibben is accurate—and I think the evidence clearly supports his assessment—then we can't pretend all that's needed is tinkering with existing systems to fix a few environmental problems; massive changes in how we live are required, what McKibben characterizes as a new kind of civilization. No matter where any one of us sits in the social and economic hierarchies, there is no escape from the dislocations that will come with such changes. Money and power might insulate some from the most wrenching consequences of these shifts, but there is no escape. We do not live in stable societies and no longer live on a stable planet. We may feel safe and secure in specific places at specific times, but it's hard to believe in any safety and security in a collective sense.

These warnings are not new. In 1992, about 1,700 of the world's leading scientists issued a warning, which began:

> Human beings and the natural world are on a collision course. Human activities inflict harsh and often irreversible damage on the environment and on critical resources.

---

28 McKibben, *Eaarth*, p. 25.

If not checked, many of our current practices put at serious risk the future that we wish for human society and the plant and animal kingdoms, and may so alter the living world that it will be unable to sustain life in the manner that we know. Fundamental changes are urgent if we are to avoid the collision our present course will bring about.[29]

Two decades later, warnings continue to be ignored. Pick a metaphor. Are we a car running out of gas? A train about to derail? A raft going over the waterfall? Whatever the choice, it's not a pretty picture.[30] Again, this kind of realization is not confined to "radical environmentalists" or "leftist revolutionaries." Consider the judgment of James Wolfensohn near the end of his term as president of the World Bank:

> It is time to take a cold, hard look at the future. Our planet is not balanced. Too few control too much, and many have too little to hope for. Too much turmoil, too many wars, too much suffering. The demographics of the future speak to a growing imbalance of people, resources, and the environment. If we act together now, we can change the world for the better. If we do not, we shall leave greater and more intractable problems for our children.[31]

---

29 Henry Kendall, a Nobel Prize physicist and former chair of the Union of Concerned Scientists' board of directors, was the primary author of the "World Scientists' Warning to Humanity." http://www.ucsusa.org/ucs/about/1992-world-scientists-warning-to-humanity.html

30 For a review of the threats, see Fred Guterl, *The Fate of the Species: Why the Human Race May Cause Its Own Extinction and How We Can Stop It* (New York: Bloomsbury, 2012).

31 James D. Wolfensohn, address to the Board of Governors of the World Bank Group, September 23, 2003. http://siteresources.worldbank.org/NEWS/Resources/jdwsp-092303.pdf

Chapter 4: The Systems of the World

Wolfenshohn's summary is clear enough, but the call to "act together" requires a shared understanding of the causes of these problems. The projects we undertake together are going to reflect our assessment of the origins of the problems. Are the targets a few "bad apples"—specific corporations or politicians who corrupt otherwise workable systems? Should we press the people in power to act more responsibly within the existing institutions, assuming that the institutions themselves are sound? Or should the basic systems be changed? Should we re-evaluate those institutions and consider whether the disastrous results were the inevitable outcome of the logic and values of the systems that created those institutions?

The focus on bad apples requires a less strenuous response, leading to calls for increased piety while continuing business-as-usual. The focus on systems demands a deeper critical self-reflection and a willingness to consider serious changes. We should choose the latter path, which is more painful but more productive. Choosing that path requires investigation into the systems most crucial in shaping the contemporary world: white supremacy, patriarchy, imperialism, capitalism, and the extractive/industrial system.

White Supremacy and Patriarchy

Discussion of race and gender are often dismissed as mere "identity politics," marked by the shallow rhetoric about multiculturalism that has become common in mainstream America and that has undermined the radical analysis of concentrated wealth and power that was once at the core of these movements. This tepid "diversity talk" leads to a focus on people of color and women jockeying for a fairer distribution of the slots within political and economic hierarchies. Making the existing institutions fairer is a good thing but isn't enough—we have to focus on a deeper critique of white supremacy and patriarchy. Those terms may seem archaic, given the advances made by civil-rights and feminist movements, but they remind us that racialized and gendered disparities in wealth and well-being remain. These problems are rooted not in the inadequacy of people of color but in white dominance, and women still face the social limitations and physical threats that come from male dominance.

Let's remember why the categories of race and gender are relevant. After all, we could divide the world into a variety of different categories, such as blue eyes v. brown eyes, made famous in Jane Elliot's classroom exercise.[32] We focus on race and gender because of their social significance, especially the discrepancies in power and wealth associated with them. We care about race and gender because of racism and sexism. Race and gender are identity categories, and if there were no meaningful consequences that flowed from those categories, then the categories would not be central to our analysis of people's lives. We care because of the racist and sexist attitudes people hold, and because of racist and sexist actions that some people engage in, resulting in injury to others. But another step remains: Where do those attitudes and behaviors come from? What are the underlying systems out of which those injuries arise? If we really care about creating a more just world, then we have to name those systems and understand how they work.

The systems that give rise to race/racism and gender/sexism are white supremacy and patriarchy. Once named, it's possible to talk about the ideological and material realities of those systems. But just getting to this point is itself an achievement. It's an important move simply to name the systems because so many in the culture want to believe that we have moved beyond white supremacy and created a "post racial" society, or that patriarchy is an old-fashioned term no longer relevant. To understand those systems within which we operate, we look at ideological underpinnings (how we come to think about the world) and material realities (how the world comes to be as a result of actions that flow from that thinking). In the previous chapter we highlighted some of those material realities. What about the way we think?

In the United States today, everyone except an overt racist acknowledges our white-supremacist past and condemns the inherent injustice of that system, though often qualifying their positions with a demand that we see those historical crimes "in context." That leads to routine denial of the extent of the genocidal campaigns against indigenous people, the degree to which U.S. economic development depended on African slave labor, the depth of the exploitation of Asian workers, and the brutal consequences of the U.S. aggression that took over Mexican territory.

Even with that hedging, white supremacy is widely understood

---

32 Frontline, "A Class Divided." http://www.pbs.org/wgbh/pages/frontline/shows/divided/.

to be a moral evil. That's why in the dominant culture, the term "white supremacist" is applied only to those overt racists, such as members of neo-Nazi groups or the Klan, and is not used to describe U.S. society as a whole. Given the achievements of a civil-rights movement that ended formal apartheid and the election of an African-American president, most people reject the claim that the United States remains a white-supremacist society. But what are the ideological realities?

Studies consistently show that white-supremacist attitudes endure, even in people who are not overtly racist. Equivalent resumes sent to employers produce higher callback rates for a job interview when the applicant has a white-sounding name rather than a black-sounding name.[33] White people watching a video of a neighborhood evaluate the quality of the place as lower if there are non-white people walking the streets compared with white people in the frame.[34] Whatever the stated beliefs of white America, racist attitudes are deeply woven into the fabric of the culture.[35]

In the United States today, patriarchy also is assumed to be a term appropriate only to describe our past or other societies today. For most of U.S. history, women were either property or second-class citizens, denied the rights of men in the political and economic arenas. The culture acknowledges that history, though underplaying the depth of the dehumanization of women during that phase of patriarchy, with its illusions about "putting women on a pedestal."

If the term "patriarchy" is heard in contemporary conversation it might be applied to fundamentalist Mormon men who reign over polygamist communities, but not to U.S. society. Given the achievements of the suffragist and women's liberation movements in the 20th century and the fact that a woman came close to winning a major party's nomination for president in the 21st century, most people reject the claim that the United States remains a patriarchal society. But what are the ideological realities?

Unlike the discourse on race, all of polite society has not renounced

---

33 Marianne Bertrand and Sendhil Mullainathan, "Are Emily and Greg More Employable than Lakisha and Jamal? A Field Experiment on Labor Market Discrimination," *American Economic Review*, 94:4 (2004): 991–1013; and Devah Pager, *Marked: Race, Crime, and Finding Work in an Era of Mass Incarceration* (Chicago: University of Chicago Press, 2007).

34 Maria Krysan, Reynolds Farley, and Mick P. Couper, "In the Eye of the Beholder: Racial Beliefs and Residential Segregation," *Du Bois Review*, 5:1 (2008): 5–26.

35 For an extended discussion, see Robert Jensen, *The Heart of Whiteness: Confronting Race, Racism and White Privilege* (San Francisco: City Lights Books, 2005).

male dominance. The term "patriarchy," with its connotations of an almost feudal status of women, may be rejected, but two forms of patriarchal ideology remain strong. One is a theological version, seen most clearly in conservative Christian circles. Men—husbands in heterosexual marriages—are seen as the natural head of a household, charged by God with leadership responsibilities. The man should exercise that power responsibly, but exercise it he must, and women find their place in that chain of command.[36] There's also a secular version of this, flowing not from belief in a divinely mandated order but from what is claimed to be the immutable reality of our evolutionary history.[37] Instead of recognizing patriarchy as a recent phenomenon, dating back no more than 10,000 years, this secular version misreads human history as being patriarchal from the start. From this view, for example, male promiscuity and sexual violence are seen as "natural" and not a product of a male-dominant culture.[38]

At the heart of radical critiques of white supremacy and patriarchy is a rejection of hierarchy in all its forms. That leads naturally to a critique of imperialism and capitalism. Empire allows the extraction of the wealth of some societies to enrich privileged people in other places. Capitalism creates a world defined by greed and attempts to reduce us all to crass maximizers of a narrowly defined self-interest.

Imperialism: Immoral, Illegal, Ineffective

The United States is the current (though fading) empire in the world, and empires are bad things. We have to let go of self-indulgent notions of American exceptionalism—the idea that the United States is a unique engine of freedom and democracy in the world and therefore responsible and benevolent. Empires throughout history have used coercion and violence to acquire a disproportionate share of the world's resources, and the U.S. empire is no different.

---

36 This was a key part of the Promise Keepers movement. See Russ Bellant, "Christian Soldiers for Theocracy," *Front Lines Research*, 1:5 (May 1995).
http://www.publiceye.org/eyes/promkeep.html

37 For a discussion of how this ideology is used in discussions of sexual violence, see Cheryl Brown Travis, ed., *Evolution, Gender, and Rape* (Cambridge, MA: MIT Press, 2003).

38 For an extended discussion, see Robert Jensen, *Getting Off: Pornography and the End of Masculinity* (Boston: South End Press, 2007).

Although the past decade's invasions of Afghanistan and Iraq are particularly brutal examples of U.S. imperial violence, none of this is new; the United States was founded by men with imperial visions who conquered the continent and then turned to the world. Most chart the beginning of the external U.S. empire-building phase with the 1898 Spanish-American War and the conquest of the Philippines that continued for some years after. That project went forward in the early 20th century, most notably in Central America, where regular U.S. military incursions made countries safe for investment, though dangerous for the aspirations of ordinary people living in those countries.

This empire emerged in full force after World War II, as the United States assumed the role of the dominant power in the world and intensified the project of subordinating the developing world to the U.S. system. Those efforts went forward under the banner of "anti-communism" until the early 1990s, but continued after the demise of the Soviet Union under various other guises, most notably the so-called "war on terrorism." Whether it was Latin America, southern Africa, the Middle East, or Southeast Asia, the central goal of U.S. foreign policy has been consistent: to make sure that an independent course of development did not succeed anywhere. The "virus" of independent development could not be allowed to take root in any country out of a fear that it might infect the rest of the developing world.[39]

The victims of this policy—the vast majority of them non-white—can be counted in the millions. In the Western Hemisphere, U.S. policy was carried out mostly through proxy armies, such as the Contras in Nicaragua in the 1980s, or support for dictatorships and military regimes that brutally repressed their own people, such as El Salvador. The result throughout the region was hundreds of thousands of dead—millions across Latin America over the course of the 20th century—and whole countries ruined.

Direct U.S. military intervention was another tool of U.S. policymakers, with the most grotesque example being the attack on Southeast Asia. After supporting the failed French effort to recolonize Vietnam after World War II, the United States invaded South Vietnam and also intervened in Laos and Cambodia, at a cost of

---

39 Noam Chomsky, *World Orders, Old and New* (New York: Columbia University Press, 1996).

3–4 million Southeast Asians dead and a region destabilized. To prevent the spread of the "virus" there, we dropped 6.5 million tons of bombs and 400,000 tons of napalm on the people of Southeast Asia. Saturation bombing of civilian areas, counterterrorism programs and political assassination, routine killings of civilians, and 11.2 million gallons of Agent Orange to destroy crops and ground cover—all were part of the U.S. attack.[40]

On 9/11/01, the vague terrorism justification for post-Cold War policy became tangible for everyone. But rather than explore the roots of the attack and bring U.S. policy in line with democratic and humanitarian rhetoric and principles, political leaders mobilized the public to support a violent response. With the U.S. economy no longer the source of dominance, policymakers used the terrorist attacks to justify an expansion of military operations in Central Asia and the Middle East. Though non-military approaches to terrorism were more viable, the rationale for ever-larger defense spending was set.

A decade later, the failures of this imperial policy are clearer than ever. U.S. foreign and military policy has always been immoral, based not on principle but on power. That policy routinely has been illegal, violating the basic tenets of international law and the constitutional system. Now, more than ever, we can see that this approach to world affairs is ineffective, no matter what criteria for effectiveness we use. An immoral and criminal policy has lost even its craven justification: It will not guarantee American dominance.

That failure is, paradoxically, the light at the end of the tunnel. As the elite bipartisan commitment to U.S. dominance fails us, citizens have a chance to demand that the United States shift to policies designed not to allow us to run the world but to help us become part of the world.

Capitalism: Inhuman, Anti-Democratic, Unsustainable

Empire-building serves an economic system, which is best described today as a predatory corporate capitalism that is inconsistent with basic human values. This description sounds odd in the United States, where so many assume that capitalism is not simply the best

---

40 Marilyn B. Young, *The Vietnam Wars, 1945–1990* (New York: HarperCollins, 1991).

among competing economic systems but the only sane and rational way to organize an economy in the contemporary world. Although the financial crisis that began in 2008 has scared many people, it has not always led to questioning the nature of the system.

The first task is to define the basics of capitalism, a socio-economic system in which (1) property, including capital assets, is owned and controlled by private persons; (2) most people must rent their labor power for money wages to survive; (3) the means of production and labor are manipulated by capitalists using rational calculation to maximize profit; and (4) most exchanges of goods and services occur through markets. "Industrial capitalism," made possible by discoveries of new energy sources, sweeping technological changes, and concentrations of capital in empires such as Great Britain, was marked by the development of the factory system and greater labor specialization and exploitation. The term "finance capitalism" is often used to mark a shift to a system in which the accumulation of profits in a financial system becomes dominant over the production processes. Increasingly, it is clear that this financialization has led not only to intensified inequality but also to greater economic instability. One of the leading economists studying inequality marks the self-destructive nature of the system:

> The financial crisis (and the world economic crisis it engendered) thus represented not so much the natural outgrowth of rising inequality as a further phase; it was the consequence of a deliberate effort to sustain a model of economic growth based on inequality that had, in the year 2000, already ended. By pressing this model past all legal and ethical limits, the United States succeeded in prolonging an "era of good feeling," and in ensuring that when the collapse came, it would utterly destroy the financial sector.[41]

Today in the United States, most people understand capitalism in the context of mass consumption—access to unprecedented levels of goods and services that are cheap enough to be affordable for ordinary people and not just elites. In such a world, everything and everyone is a commodity in the market. Within this dominant

---

41 James K. Galbraith, *Inequality and Instability: A Study of the World Economy Just Before the Great Crisis* (New York: Oxford University Press, 2012), p. 293.

ideology of market fundamentalism, it's assumed that the most extensive use of markets possible, along with privatization of many publicly owned assets and the shrinking of public services, will unleash maximal competition and result in the greatest good—and all this is inherently just, no matter what the results. If such a system creates a world in which most people live in poverty, that is taken not as evidence of a problem with market fundamentalism but evidence that fundamentalist principles have not been imposed with sufficient vigor; it is an article of faith that the "invisible hand" of the market always provides the preferred result, no matter how awful the consequences may be for people.

How to critique capitalism in such a society? We can start by pointing out that capitalism is fundamentally inhuman, anti-democratic, and unsustainable.[42]

Inhuman: The theory behind contemporary capitalism explains that because we are greedy, self-interested animals, a viable economic system must reward greedy, self-interested behavior. That's certainly part of human nature, but we also just as obviously are capable of compassion and selflessness. We can act competitively and aggressively, but we also have the capacity to act out of solidarity and cooperation—human nature is wide-ranging. In situations where compassion and solidarity are the norm, we tend to act that way. In situations where competitiveness and aggression are rewarded, most people tend toward such behavior.

Why must we accept an economic system that undermines the most decent aspects of our nature and strengthens the cruelest? Because, we're told, that's just the way people are. What evidence is there of that? Look around, we're told, at how people behave. Everywhere we look, we see greed and the pursuit of self-interest. So the proof that these greedy, self-interested aspects of our nature are dominant is that, when forced into a system that rewards greed and self-interested behavior, people often act that way. Doesn't that seem just a bit circular? A bit perverse?

Anti-democratic: In the real world—not in the textbooks or fantasies of economics professors—capitalism has always been, and will always be, a wealth-concentrating system. If you concentrate wealth in a society, you concentrate power; there is no historical example

---

42 This is adapted from Robert Jensen, *All My Bones Shake: Seeking a Progressive Path to the Prophetic Voice* (Berkeley, CA: Soft Skull Press, 2009).

to the contrary.

For all the trappings of formal democracy in the contemporary United States, everyone understands that for the most part, the wealthy dictate the basic outlines of the public policies that are put into practice by elected officials. This is cogently explained by political scientist Thomas Ferguson's "investment theory of political parties," which identifies powerful investors rather than unorganized voters as the dominant force in campaigns and elections. Ferguson describes political parties in the United States as "blocs of major investors who coalesce to advance candidates representing their interests" and that "political parties dominated by large investors try to assemble the votes they need by making very limited appeals to particular segments of the potential electorate." There can be competition between these blocs, but "on all issues affecting the vital interests that major investors have in common, no party competition will take place."[43] Whatever we might call such a system, it's not democracy in any meaningful sense of the term.

People can and do resist the system's attempt to sideline them, and an occasional politician joins the fight, but such resistance takes extraordinary effort. Those who resist sometimes win victories, some of them inspiring, but to date concentrated wealth continues to dominate. Recent expansions of corporations' ability to claim constitutional rights has further entrenched that domination.[44] If we define democracy as a system that gives ordinary people a meaningful way to participate in the formation of public policy, rather than just a role in ratifying decisions made by the powerful, then it's clear that capitalism and democracy are mutually exclusive.

Unsustainable: Capitalism is a system based on an assumption of continuing, unlimited growth—on a finite planet. There are only two ways out of this problem. We can hold out hope that we might hop over to a new planet soon, or we can embrace technological fundamentalism (more on that later) and believe that evermore complex technologies will allow us to transcend those physical limits here. Both those positions are equally delusional. Delusions may bring temporary comfort, but they don't solve problems; in fact,

---

43 Thomas Ferguson, *Golden Rule: The Investment Theory of Party Competition and the Logic of Money-Driven Political Systems* (Chicago: University of Chicago Press, 1995), pp. 27–28.
44 Jeff Clements, *Corporations Are Not People: Why They Have More Rights Than You Do and What You Can Do About It* (San Francisco, CA: Berrett-Koehler, 2012).

they tend to cause more problems, and in this world those problems keep piling up.

Critics have compared capitalism to cancer. The inhuman and anti-democratic features of capitalism mean that, like a cancer, the death system will eventually destroy the living host. Both the human communities and non-human living world that play host to capitalism eventually will be destroyed by capitalism. Capitalism is not, of course, the only unsustainable system that humans have devised, but it is the most obviously unsustainable system, and it's the one in which we are stuck. It's the one that we are told is inevitable and natural, like the air we breathe. But the air that we are breathing is choking the most vulnerable in the world, choking us, choking the planet.

Extractive/Industrial Model: Mining the World to Death

The final hierarchal system—and in some ways the most dangerous—is the industrial model of human development, the latest and most intense version of an unsustainable extractive economy.

The bounty that makes contemporary mass consumption possible did not, of course, drop out of the sky. It was ripped out of the ground and drawn from the water in a fashion that has left the continent ravaged, a dismemberment of nature that is an unavoidable consequence of a worldview that glorifies domination. "From [Europeans'] first arrival we have behaved as though nature must be either subdued or ignored," writes the scientist and philosopher Wes Jackson, one of the leading thinkers in the sustainable agriculture movement.[45] As Jackson points out, our economy has always been extractive, even before the industrial revolution dramatically accelerated the assault in the 19th century and the petrochemical revolution began poisoning the world more intensively in the 20th. We mined the forests, soil, and aquifers, just as we eventually mined minerals and fossil fuels, leaving ecosystems ragged and in ruin, perhaps beyond recovery in any human timeframe. All that was done by people who believed in their right to dominate.

One way to understand that domination is the context of the two major revolutions in human history—the agricultural and industrial revolutions.

---

45 Wes Jackson, *Becoming Native to This Place* (Lexington: University Press of Kentucky, 1994), p. 19.

The agricultural revolution started about 10,000 years ago when a gathering-hunting species discovered how to cultivate plants for food and domesticate animals. Two crucial things resulted from that, one ecological and one political. Ecologically, the invention of agriculture kicked off an intensive human assault on natural systems. Gathering-hunting humans were capable of damaging a local ecosystem, but the large-scale destruction we cope with today has its origins in agriculture when humans began exhausting the energy-rich carbon of the soil, what Jackson has described as the first step in the entrenchment of an extractive economy and Jared Diamond has called "the worst mistake in human history."[46] Human agricultural practices vary from place to place but have never been sustainable over the long term. Politically, the ability to stockpile food made possible concentrations of power and resulting hierarchies that were foreign to gathering-hunting societies. Again, this is not to say that humans were not capable of doing bad things to each other prior to agriculture, but only that what we understand, as large-scale institutionalized oppression has its roots in agriculture. We need not romanticize pre-agricultural life to recognize the ways in which agriculture made possible dramatically different levels of unsustainability and injustice.

The industrial revolution that began in the last half of the 18th century in Great Britain intensified the magnitude of the human assault on ecosystems. Unleashing the concentrated energy of coal, oil, and natural gas to run a machine-based world has produced unparalleled material comfort for some. Whatever one thinks of the effect of such comforts on human psychology (and, in my view, the effect has been mixed), the processes that produce the comfort are destroying the capacity of the ecosphere to sustain human life as we know it into the future, and in the present those comforts are not distributed in a fashion that is consistent with any meaningful conception of justice. The ecological consequences of this revolution are painfully obvious.

These two changes in human history come together today in what typically is called "industrial agriculture," the dominant method of producing food at this moment in history in the United States, the rest of the developed world, and increasingly in the developing

---

46 Jared Diamond, "The Worst Mistake in the History of the Human Race," *Discover Magazine*, May 1987, pp. 64–66.

world. It is a style of agriculture that everyone agrees has produced substantial increases in yields, tripling the world grain harvest in the second half of the 20th century. Critics, however, point out that those yields have come at the cost of deep, and possibly permanent, injuries to the land, people, and other species.[47]

Various characteristics of industrial agriculture have been evolving over time, but by the second half of the 20th century the industrial system was firmly in place in the United States. The features of the current system include: (1) heavy use of nonrenewable inputs purchased off the farm, such as chemical fertilizers, pesticides, and herbicides; (2) extensive mechanization, making farming both capital- and technology-intensive; (3) heavy reliance on fossil fuels for those inputs and mechanization, to such an extent that critics joke that modern farming is the use of land to covert petroleum into food; (4) decreased self-sufficiency for individuals and communities, and increased dependence on corporations; and (5) a lack of concern for, if not outright hostility toward, systems and living things that do not directly contribute to production.

Along with the dramatic increases in food production, the predictable results of this system have been: (1) drastic and continuing loss of topsoil; (2) declining soil fertility; (3) a severe reduction in farm population; and (4) the resulting loss of knowledge of traditional methods that require fewer inputs, less technology, less capital, and more people.[48] This is what Jackson calls "the failure of success," the paradox of a system that results in more food coming from fields that have less, and less fertile, soil.[49] The so-called "Green Revolution"—a variety of research and social programs associated with the work of Nobel Prize-winning agronomist Norman Borlaug—was not really a revolution but an extension of industrial agriculture to the Third World, which resulted in short-term reductions in hunger but also exported this extremely fragile model to the developing world, creating the same long-term problems.

The agricultural revolution produced the first systematic extractive model, which set us on a road to eventual collapse. The industrial revolution ramped up our speed. The material benefits of those

---

47 Wendell Berry, *The Unsettling of America: Culture and Agriculture*, 3rd ed. (San Francisco: Sierra Club Books, 1996).
48 Wes Jackson, *Consulting the Genius of the Place: An Ecological Approach to a New Agriculture.* (Berkeley, CA: Counterpoint, 2010).
49 Wes Jackson, *New Roots for Agriculture* (Lincoln: University of Nebraska Press, 1980), p. 14.

revolutions are not spread equally or equitably around the world,[50] which challenges us to create a more just world as we struggle to find a new model for a sustainable world.

50 Raj Patel, *Stuffed and Starved: The Hidden Battle for the World Food System* (Brooklyn, NY: Melville House, 2008).

Chapter 5:
Reasonable Responses

The first step in dealing with a difficult situation is to muster the courage to face it honestly, to assess the actual depth and severity of a problem and identify the systems from which the problem emerges. The existing social, economic, and political systems produce a distribution of wealth and well-being that is inconsistent with moral principles, as the ecological capital of the planet is drawn down faster than it can regenerate. The systems that structure almost all human societies produce profoundly unjust and fundamentally unsustainable results. We have both a moral obligation and practical reasons to work for justice and sustainability.

We need first to imagine, and then begin to create, alternative systems that will reduce inequality and slow, and we hope eventually reverse, the human assault on the ecosphere. To work toward those goals, individuals can (and should) make changes in their personal lives to consume less; corporations can (and should) be subject to greater regulation; and the most corrupt political leaders can (and should) be turned out of office. But those limited efforts, while noble and important in the short term, are inadequate to address the problems if no systemic and structural changes are made.

That sounds difficult because it will be, and glib slogans can't change that fact. A longstanding cliché of progressive politics—organizers' task is to "make it easy for people to do the right thing"—is inadequate in these circumstances. Given the depth of the dysfunction, it will not be easy to do the right thing. It will, in fact, be very hard, and there's no sense pretending otherwise. At this point in history, anything that is easy and can be achieved quickly is almost certainly insufficient and likely irrelevant in the long run. Attempting to persuade people that large-scale social change will come easily is not only insulting to their intelligence but is guaranteed to fail. If organizers can persuade people to join a movement based on promises of victories that won't disrupt privileged lives—victories that cannot be achieved—the backlash is likely worse than the status quo.

There's one simple reason that serious change cannot be easy: We are the first species in the history of the planet that is going to have to will itself to practice restraint across the board, especially in our use of energy. Like other carbon-based creatures, we evolved to pursue energy-rich carbon, not constrain ourselves. Going against that basic fact of nature will not be easy.

Modern humans—animals like us, with our brain capacity—have been on the planet about 200,000 years, which means that we've lived within the hierarchical systems launched by agriculture for only about 5 percent of human history. We are living today in a world defined by systems in which we did not evolve as a species and to which we are still struggling to adapt. What today we take to be normal ways of organizing human societies—nation-states with capitalist economies—are recent developments, radically different than how we lived for 95 percent of our evolutionary history. We evolved in small gatherer-hunter groups, band-level societies that were basically egalitarian. Research on human social networks suggest that there is a limit on the "natural" size of a human social group of about 150 members, which is determined by our cognitive capacity. This has been called "Dunbar's number" (after anthropologist Robin Dunbar)—the number of individuals with whom any one of us can maintain stable relationships.[51] In that world, we pursed that energy-rich carbon without the knowledge or technology that makes that same pursuit so dangerous today.

So we are, as Wes Jackson puts it, "a species out of context."[52] We are living in a world that is in many ways dramatically out of sync with the kind of animals we are. If we are to create systems and structures that will make possible an ongoing human presence on the planet, we have to understand our evolutionary history and adapt our institutions to reflect our essentially local existence—people live, after all, not on "the planet" but in a specific place, as part of an ecosystem—on a scale and with a scope that we are capable of managing. But we also have to acknowledge that we are inextricably connected to others around the world because of more recent history. As a result of the centuries of imperialism that have advantaged some and disadvantaged others, we are all morally connected, as well as literally connected by modern transportation and communication technology. The task is not to go backward to some imagined Eden, but to understand our history to create a more just and sustainable future.

This means we have to recognize that the biological processes that govern the larger living world, along with our own evolu-

---

51 Robin Dunbar, *The Human Story* (London: Faber and Faber, 2004).
52 Wes Jackson, "The Ecosystem as a Conceptual Tool for Agriculture and Culture," 1996. http://www.landinstitute.org/vnews/display.v/ART/1996/06/01/3aa3e2fe9

tionary history, impose limits on human societies. Either we start shaping our world to reflect those limits so that we can control to some degree the dramatic changes coming, or we will be reacting to changes that can't be controlled. That isn't an easy task; as James Howard Kunstler points out, "the only thing that complex societies have not been able to do is contract, to become smaller and less complex, and to do it in a programmatic way that reduces the pain of transition."[53] Though history suggests that "people do what they can until they can't," it's still imperative that we face the challenge:

> Our longer-term destination is a society run at much lower levels of available energy, with much lower populations, and a time-out from the kinds of progressive innovation that so many have taken for granted their whole lives. It was an illusory result of a certain sequencing in the exploitation of resources in the planet earth that we have now pretty much run through. We have an awful lot to contend with in this reset of human activities.[54]

If there is to be a decent future, we have to give up on the imperial fantasy of endless power, the capitalist fantasy of endless growth, the technological fantasy of endless comfort. Those systems have long been celebrated as the engines of unprecedented wealth, albeit for a limited segment of the world's population. Instead of celebrating, we should mourn the world that these systems have created and search for something better. Systems that celebrate domination are death cults, not the basis for societies striving for justice and sustainability.

Our task can be stated simply: We seek justice, the simple plea for decent lives for all, and sustainability, a balance in which human social systems can thrive within the larger living world. Justice and sustainability have a common economics, politics, ethics, and theology behind them—rooted in a rejection of concentrated power and hierarchy—but there is no cookbook we can pull off the shelf with a recipe for success. We can articulate principles, identify rough guidelines, and search for specific solutions to immediate problems.

On justice: Our philosophical and theological systems all

---

53 Kunstler, *Too Much Magic*, p. 188.
54 Ibid., p. 196.

acknowledge the inherent dignity of all human beings. We say that we believe that all people are equal, though we accept conditions in the world in which all people cannot live with dignity, where any claim of equality is a farce. In that case we understand the principles but do not live accordingly.

On sustainability: There is less consensus on the philosophy and theology on which we ground a concern for sustainability. Is it purely pragmatic? Do we need to conserve the world to sustain ourselves? Should we have some more expansive concern about the non-human living world? Do other living things have a claim on us? There are no simple or obvious answers. We may have some general reverence for all life, but most of us value the lives of our children, our friends, and other humans more than we value the lives of other animals. But even with a lack of clarity about how to value various forms of life, we have to understand that we are part of that larger living world and that we should be careful about how we carve it up into categories.

For example, we should be careful not to value the pristine and ignore the human-built. We should not value the part of a forest that is untouched by human hands more than the part that has been cleared for human shelter. It is seductive to label wilderness as sacred and development as profane. Instead we should learn to see all the world—the last stands of old-growth redwoods in northern California and the most burned-out block of the South Bronx—as sacred ground. Until we do that, we have little hope of saving the former from destruction or restoring the latter to health. At its core, sustainability is about the acknowledgment of interdependence: the interdependence of people on each other, of people and other animals, of all living species and the non-living earth. We must see the interdependence of the redwoods and the South Bronx.

Again, no one has a blueprint for creating a just and sustainable society, but here is a list of a few basic assumptions and assertions that make justice and sustainability imaginable: (1) nature is not something humans have a right, divine or natural, to subdue and exploit; (2) for most of human beings' evolutionary history, our social systems encouraged the solidarity and cooperation required for survival, and our social systems today should foster those same values, (3) systems that place profit above other values inevitably cause problems they cannot solve; (4) solutions must be holistic, linking the always interdependent parts of a system, such as producers and consumers; (5) technology is not automatically beneficial and must be scrutinized before being used; and, perhaps most importantly, (6) humans have the moral and intellectual capacity to make choices that will preserve rather than destroy the larger living world.

That human capacity to choose wisely does not guarantee we always will. The ease with which intellectuals can be co-opted is a reminder of that.

Chapter 6:
Intellectuals' Failures

Given the considerable resources in the United States spent to subsidize intellectual work, why are so many intellectuals not critiquing these institutions and not highlighting the consequences of these systems? Why are so many intellectuals instead providing support for the institutions and systems? Why is the majority of intellectual work in the United States not challenging but instead helping to prop up the unjust distribution of wealth and power, and the unsustainable extractive/industrial system? Both intellectuals and the people who provide the resources that allow intellectuals to work should ponder this crucial question.

I am not suggesting that to be a responsible intellectual one must agree with me on all these issues, that anyone who does not agree with my approach to these issues is a soulless sell-out. My argument is that if we take seriously the basic moral principles at the core of modern philosophical and theological systems we claim to believe in, in light of the data on social injustice and the serious threats to ecological sustainability, these questions should be central in the work of intellectuals. Based on my experience as a journalist, professor, and political activist—a life in which I have always worked in intellectual professions and interacted with many other intellectuals in various settings—I have learned that the story is complicated but that a sharp critique of intellectuals as a social formation is warranted.

First, let's recognize that intellectual work generally comes with considerable privilege. That does not mean that intellectuals don't work hard, make sacrifices, or feel stress. But in general, intellectuals are compensated well for work that is not physically hazardous and can be rewarding on many levels. There are many intellectuals-in-training (graduate students) and underemployed intellectuals (adjunct faculty) who face overwhelming workloads and few perks, and so we should be cautious about generalizing too much about the category of "intellectual." This analysis focuses on those doing intellectual work with the most privilege and the most autonomy.

Ideally, we pay intellectuals to help us deepen our understanding of how the world works, toward the goal of shaping a world more consistent with our moral and political principles, and our collective self-interest. What are the forces that keep people, especially relatively privileged people, mute in the face of such a clear need for critical intellectual work? The first, and easiest, answer is individual self-interest—the status and economic rewards that come to intellectuals who serve power. Upton Sinclair put it most succinctly: "It is difficult to get a man to understand something, when his salary depends upon his not understanding it."[55]

No doubt some intellectuals make calculations about how to use their abilities to enrich themselves, but in my experience such crass greed is relatively rare. I suspect that a desire to be accepted by peers is at least as powerful a motivation for intellectuals to accept the status quo. Humans are social animals who generally seek a safe and secure place in a social group, and there's no reason intellectuals would be different. Even when concentrated wealth and power do not threaten people with serious punishments, the desire to be a well-regarded member of an intellectual community is a powerful conformity-inducer. When one's professional cohort works within the worldview that the wealthy and powerful construct, the boundaries of that world seem appropriate. Curiosity about what lies beyond those boundaries tends to atrophy.

Those forces have been in play for a long time, but another potentially crucial factor is the way in which confronting the reality of injustice and unsustainability can be morally and psychologically overwhelming for anyone. As the documentation of human suffering and the threats to ecological sustainability accumulate, in an era when multiple communication channels make it easy to be aware of more and more of this information, that awareness can seem to be too much to face. The desire to rationalize the suffering and imagine an easy escape is easy to understand.

Rationalization #1: Justifying Hierarchy

When humans suffer in extreme situations, such as war or natural disasters, most people in most situations find it easy to care and respond. When the suffering is ongoing and apparently endemic to the systems of the world, staying connected to that suffering is more difficult. In such situations, it can be attractive to find ways to justify hierarchy and the resulting suffering, rather than to challenge power.

There is wide consensus on the values that are central to constructing a decent human society: justice, equality, compassion, honesty, opportunity, sharing. It is difficult to imagine such a society

---

55 Upton Sinclair, *I, Candidate for Governor: And How I Got Licked* (Berkeley: University of California Press, 1935/1994), p. 109.

without these basic elements: (1) the belief in the inherent dignity of all human beings; (2) a sense of solidarity with at least those in one's community, if not beyond; and (3) a commitment to achieving a rough equality so that everyone has access to the material requirements for a decent life. That list does not assume that people are morally perfect or perfectible, but instead articulates common aspirations for ourselves, others, and society.

How do we explain the fact that most people's stated philosophical and theological systems are rooted in concepts of equality, solidarity, and the inherent dignity of all people, yet we allow violence, exploitation, and oppression to flourish? Only a small percentage of people in any given society are truly sociopaths, those who engage in cruel and oppressive behavior openly and without a capacity for empathy. In my experience, the most common way in which people make their peace with that contradiction is to accept the claim that hierarchy and injustice are inevitable, and that the best we can do is try to smooth off the rough edges of such systems. The process can be summed up like this:

—The systems and structures in which we live are hierarchical.
—Hierarchical systems and structures deliver to those in the dominant class certain privileges, pleasures, and material benefits.
—People are typically hesitant to give up such privileges, pleasures, and benefits.
—But, those benefits clearly come at the expense of those in the subordinated class.
—Given the widespread acceptance of basic notions of dignity, solidarity, and equality, the existence of hierarchy has to be justified in some way other than crass self-interest.
—One of the most persuasive arguments for systems of domination and subordination is that they are "natural."

So, oppressive systems work hard to make it appear that the hierarchy—and the disparity in power and resources that flow from hierarchy—is natural and, therefore, beyond modification. If white people are naturally smarter and more virtuous than people of color, then white supremacy is inevitable and justifiable. If men are naturally stronger and more capable of leadership than women, then patriarchy is inevitable and justifiable. If rich people are naturally

clearer-thinking and harder-working than poor people, then economic inequality is inevitable and justifiable. If the strong are, well,
stronger than the weak, then the strong will rule.

As John Stuart Mill noted in his argument for women's rights,
"Was there ever any domination which did not appear natural to
those who possessed it?"[56] For unjust hierarchies, and the illegiti-
mate authority that is exercised in them, maintaining their naturalness is essential. Not surprisingly, people in the dominant class
exercising the power gravitate easily to such a view. And because
of their power to control key intellectual institutions (especially
education and mass communication), those in the dominant class
can fashion a story about the world that leads some portion of the
people in the subordinated class to internalize the ideology. A social
order that violates almost everyone's basic principles is transformed
into a natural order that cannot be changed.

Rationalization #2: Celebrating Technology

Facing the ecological realities is even more overwhelming. People
once spoke of "environmental problems" that seemed limited and
manageable, but now the questions are about whether a large-scale
human presence on the planet will be viable within the foresee-
able future. An honest assessment of the state of the ecosphere is
frightening, and it is easier to believe that the world's systems can
magically continue rather than thinking about how radical changes
in those systems are necessary—and how even with such radical
changes there is no guarantee that we can avoid catastrophe.

That frightening possibility is why the culture in general, and
intellectuals in particular, are quick to embrace technological fundamentalism, a form of magical thinking that promises a way out
of the problems that the extractive/industrial economy has created. Technological fundamentalists believe that the increasing
use of evermore sophisticated high-energy advanced technology
is always a good thing and that any problems caused by the unintended consequences of such technology eventually can be rem-
edied by more technology. Perhaps the ultimate example of this is
"geo-engineering," the belief that we can intervene at the planetary

---

56 John Stuart Mill, *The Subjection of Women* (New York: D. Appleton and Company, 1869), p. 21.

level in the climate system to deal effectively with global warming. Given massive human failure at much lower levels of intervention, this approach—which "offers the tantalizing promise of a climate change fix that would allow us to continue our resource-exhausting way of life, indefinitely"[57]—is, quite literally, insane.

Those who question such "solutions" are often said to be anti-technology, which is a meaningless insult. All human beings use technology of some kind, whether stone tools or computers. An anti-fundamentalist position does not assert that all technology is bad, but that the introduction of new technology should be evaluated carefully on the basis of its effects—predictable and unpredictable—on human communities and the non-human world, with an understanding of the limits of our knowledge. We have moved too far and too fast, outstripping our capacity to manage the world we have created. The answer is not some naïve return to a romanticized past, but a recognition of what we have created and a systematic evaluation to determine how to recover from our most dangerous missteps.

But the technological fundamentalists see no reason to consider such things. They have faith in human cleverness. The title of a recent book by an environmentalist—*The God Species: Saving the Planet in the Age of Humans*[58]—sums it up: Technological fundamentalists believe humans can play God and control an infinitely complex universe with enough competence to save not only ourselves but the planet. There's nothing new about that arrogance. In 1968, Stewart Brand began the *Whole Earth Catalog* with that famous line, "We are as gods and might as well get good at it."[59] Four decades later, with the evidence of human failure piling up, Brand remained the loyal technological fundamentalist, arguing that his suggestion had become an imperative: "We are as gods and HAVE to get good at it."[60]

Our experience with the unintended consequences of modern technology is fairly extensive. For example, there's the case of automobiles and the burning of petroleum in internal-combustion engines, which give us the ability to travel considerable distances

---

57 Naomi Klein, "Geoengineering: Testing the Waters," *New York Times*, October 28, 2012. http://www.nytimes.com/2012/10/28/opinion/sunday/geoengineering-testing-the-waters.html?_r=1&&pagewanted=all

58 Mark Lynas, *The God Species: Saving the Planet in the Age of Humans* (Washington, DC: National Geographic Society, 2011).

59 http://www.wholeearth.com/issue/1010/article/196/the.purpose.of.the.whole.earth.catalog

60 Stewart Brand, *Whole Earth Discipline: An Ecopragmatist Manifesto* (New York: Viking Adult, 2009), p. 1.

with a fair amount of individual autonomy. This technology also has given us traffic jams and road rage, strip malls and smog, while contributing to rapid climate change that threatens sustainable life on the planet. We haven't quite figured out how to cope with these problems, and in retrospect it might have been wise to go slower in the development of a system geared toward private, individual transportation based on the car and spend more time considering potential consequences.

Or how about CFCs and the ozone hole? Chlorofluorocarbons have a variety of industrial, commercial, and household applications, including in air conditioning. They were thought to be a miracle chemical when introduced in the 1930s—non-toxic, non-flammable, and non-reactive with other chemical compounds. But in the 1980s, researchers began to understand that while CFCs are stable in the troposphere, when they move to the stratosphere and are broken down by strong ultraviolet light they release chlorine atoms that deplete the ozone layer. This unintended effect deflated the exuberance a bit. Depletion of the ozone layer means that more UV radiation reaches the Earth's surface, and overexposure to UV radiation is a cause of skin cancer, cataracts, and immune suppression.

But wait, the technological fundamentalists might argue, our experience with CFCs refutes your argument—humans got a handle on that one and banned CFCs, and now the ozone hole is closing. These gases, which were once commonly used in air-conditioning, were regulated in 1987 through the Montreal Protocol, which has reduced damage to the ozone layer. The oldest and most damaging CFC coolants have been largely eliminated from use, and the newer hydrochlorofluorocarbons that are now widely used have little or no effect on the ozone layer. That's all true, but unfortunately we now know that the HCFC gases contribute to global warming. Scientists estimate that up to a quarter of all global warming will be attributable to those gases by 2050, so that "the therapy to cure one global environmental disaster is now seeding another."[61]

So the reasonable question is: If the dangerous HCFCs that replaced the dangerous CFCs are replaced by a new chemical that appears harmless, how long will it take before the dangerous effects

---

61 Elisabeth Rosenthal and Andrew W. Lehren, "Relief in Every Window, but Global Worry Too," *New York Times*, June 20, 2012. http://www.nytimes.com/2012/06/21/world/asia/global-demand-for-air-conditioning-forces-tough-environmental-choices.html?pagewanted=all

of that replacement become visible? There's no way to predict, but it seems reasonable to ask the question. Society didn't react to the news about CFCs or HCFCs by thinking about ways to step back from a developed world that has become dependent on air conditioning, but instead continues to search for replacements to keep the air conditioning running.[62]

Intellectuals are in the business of assessing problems and offering solutions. Technological fundamentalism allows intellectuals to offer solutions that don't threaten existing institutions and don't make demands on society in general, which allows intellectuals to retain their status and level of comfort, at least in the short term. The obvious problem is that if we look only for "solutions" that don't disturb existing systems, and those existing systems are unsustainable, then our solutions are at best irrelevant and at worst will exacerbate the fundamental problems and make it harder for people to imagine new systems.

This is not an argument to abandon all attempts to improve technology, stop exploring ways technology can contribute to a healthier planet, or halt research on renewable energy. A sensible approach to our cascading ecological crises is to pursue multiple strategies that mitigate the worst of what exists today while planning for a radically different tomorrow. Technological fundamentalism is dangerous because it encourages us to focus on the former and ignore the latter.

The problem, succinctly stated: When intellectuals limit themselves to inquiry that stays safely within existing systems, they are being unrealistic. That claim turns the tables on establishment intellectuals, who routinely criticize more radical colleagues for not being realistic. But imagine that you are riding comfortably on a train. You look out the window and see that not too far ahead the tracks end abruptly and that the train will derail if it continues moving ahead. You suggest that the train should stop immediately and that the passengers go forward on foot. This will require a major shift in everyone's way of traveling, of course, but it appears to you to be the only realistic option; to continue barreling forward is to guarantee catastrophic consequences. But when you propose this course of action, others who have grown comfortable riding on the

---

62 Stan Cox, a leading researcher in sustainable agriculture, explains how we can reduce our reliance on air-conditioning in *Losing Our Cool: Uncomfortable Truths About Our Air-Conditioned World (and Finding New Ways to Get Through the Summer)* (New York: New Press, 2010).

train say, "Everybody likes riding the train, and so telling us to get off is not realistic."

In the contemporary United States, we are trapped in a similar delusion. We are told that it is "realistic" to capitulate to the absurd idea that the systems in which we live are the only systems possible because some people like them and wish them to continue. But what if our current level of First-World consumption is exhausting the ecological basis for life? Too bad; the only "realistic" options are those that take that lifestyle as non-negotiable. What if real democracy is not possible in a nation-state with 300 million people? Too bad; the only "realistic" options are those that take this way of organizing a polity as immutable. What if the hierarchies on which our lives are based are producing extreme material deprivation for subordinated people and a kind of dull misery among the privileged? Too bad; the only "realistic" options are those that accept hierarchy as inevitable.

The ultimate test of our intellectual abilities is whether we can face the possibility that there may be no way out of these traps and yet continue to work for a more just and sustainable world (more on that later). That is not easy, but to be a responsible intellectual is to be willing to get apocalyptic, and the first step in that process is to give up on the myth of neutrality. Intellectuals shouldn't claim to be neutral, and the public shouldn't take such claims seriously.

Chapter 7:
The Myth of the
Neutral Intellectual

How does the intellectual world deal with the tension between the potential for resistance to wealth and power that exists in a relatively free and open intellectual arena, and the demands of the wealthy and powerful? How does the system minimize the possibility that intellectuals will bite the hands that feed them by challenging the people and institutions that provide the resources for much of the intellectual work that gets done?

The rules of life in authoritarian and totalitarian states are clear. The state—which represents the interests of a particular set of elites—governs through a combination of coercion and violence that typically is quite brutal, and propaganda that typically is heavy-handed. In that formula, intellectuals have a clear role: Serve the state by articulating values and describing social, political, and economic forces in a fashion consistent with state power and its ideology. To the degree one does that, one will be rewarded. The Soviet Union was perhaps the paradigm case of this kind of system.

Methods of social control are more complex in a contemporary liberal, pluralist, capitalist democracy such as the United States. The state—which represents the interests of a particular group of elites—still maintains a monopoly on violence and uses it when necessary to maintain control. But because of the nature of the system and the advances made by popular movements in the past century, the state cannot rule simply by force or crude propaganda. Those who rule also realize that one advantage of a relatively open society is the dynamic, creative intellectual climate that produces innovation. To elites, that innovation is desirable in certain realms (especially the sciences, both pure and applied) but potentially dangerous in other realms (especially the humanities and social sciences). How to encourage innovation in one arena but discourage it in the other? This requires a more sophisticated management of ideology and the institutions that reproduce and transmit that ideology.

As a result, intellectuals in the contemporary United States do not face the crude choices—subordinate yourself to the state or risk serious punishment, including death—that intellectuals in more authoritarian states face. While dissident intellectuals in the United States are not always treated well—they may risk not being able to find permanent employment in an officially recognized institution, for example—they are not at this point in history routinely subject to serious consequences. One caveat to that: While that is true for those from the more privileged sectors of society, there are contemporary examples of harsh treatment for others. For example, Sami Al-Arian, a tenured Palestinian computer science professor at the University of South Florida, was vilified in the mass media and fired in December 2001 for his political views. In 2003 he was indicted by the U.S. government on charges that he used an academic think-tank at USF and an Islamic charity as fronts to raise money for the Palestinian Islamic Jihad. Prosecutors have used a variety of legal tactics to keep Al-Arian jailed or on house arrest.[63]

So, in a liberal, pluralist, capitalist democracy, the elites in the state and the corporation need intellectuals in some arenas to innovate, while in other arenas they need intellectuals to articulate values and accounts of reality that will support the system of concentrated power. What if some of those intellectuals come to a critique of that concentration of power? What if instead of articulating values in support of that power, intellectuals articulate other values? Even worse to those with power, what if those intellectuals use their privilege not only to talk about such things but to engage in political activity to change the nature of the system and the distribution of power?

Enter the myth of the neutral professional, as a way to neutralize professionals. The shift from the term "intellectual" to "professional" highlights how the myth of neutrality works in specific occupational groups, especially journalists and university professors, two of the most important intellectual positions in this society (and the two jobs I've held in my adult life).

In the political and philosophical sense in which I use the term here, neutrality is impossible. In any situation, there exists a distribution of power. To either endorse or contest that distribution is a political choice. But to take no explicit position by claiming to be neutral, which places one on the side of the status quo, is also a political choice. Myles Horton, the founder of the Highlander Folk School in Tennessee and a legendary figure in progressive organizing and adult education, is one of many who have critiqued the act of claiming neutrality, which he described as "an immoral act." Neutrality, he said, is "a code word for the existing system. It has nothing to do with anything but agreeing to what is and will always be—that's what neutrality is. Neutrality is just following the crowd.

---

63 Glenn Greenwald, "Personalizing civil liberties abuses," Salon, April 16, 2012. http://www.salon.com/2012/04/16/personalizing_civil_liberties_abuses/

Neutrality is just being what the system asks us to be."[64]

This same insight lies behind the title of historian Howard Zinn's political/intellectual memoir, *You Can't Be Neutral on a Moving Train.*[65] If a train is moving down the track, you can't plop down in a car that is part of that train and pretend to be sitting still; you're moving with the train. Likewise, a society is moving in a certain direction—power is distributed in a certain way, leading to certain kinds of institutions and relationships, which distribute the resources of the society in certain ways. We can't pretend that by sitting still—by claiming to be neutral—we can avoid accountability for our roles (which will vary according to people's place in the system). A claim of neutrality means simply that you aren't taking a position on that distribution of power and its consequences, which is a passive acceptance of the existing distribution. That is a political choice.

In the contemporary United States, professionals who want to be taken seriously in the mainstream political/intellectual culture (and have a chance at the status that comes with that) are encouraged to accept and replicate the dominant ideology, especially the central claims about: (1) the benevolence of the United States in foreign policy (the notion that the United States, alone among nations in history, pursues a policy rooted in a desire to spread freedom and democracy) and (2) the naturalness of capitalism (the notion that capitalism is not only the most efficient system, but the only sane and moral economic system). At the same time, those same professionals are encouraged in their official capacities to be politically neutral when it comes to actively promoting specific policies within the existing system or specific politicians who should run it. No one is supposed to notice that the highly politicized questions about the coherence or morality of the existing systems have been rendered invisible.

People who accept and work within the dominant ideology are not automatically wrong or corrupt; reasonable people can disagree about how best to understand and analyze complex systems. My point is simply that no one can claim to be neutral. Those of us who routinely critique the dominant view are political; the political positions we have come to hold certainly have an effect on the

---

64 Myles Horton and Paulo Freire, *We Make the Road by Walking: Conversations on Education and Social Change* (Philadelphia: Temple University Press, 1990), p. 102.
65 Howard Zinn, *You Can't Be Neutral on a Moving Train: A Personal History of Our Times* (Boston: Beacon Press, 1994).

conclusions we reach—but no more and no less than people who don't critique. That is not to say that journalism or university teaching is nothing but the imposition of one's political predispositions on reporting/writing or research/teaching, but simply to observe that all of us have a politics that affects our intellectual work. The appropriate question isn't "are you political?" but "can you defend the assumptions you make and the conclusions you reach?"

To return to the train metaphor: When we ride on trains, we typically conform to the system. The trains run on a certain schedule to certain destinations. Once a person decides to take the train, it's understandable why we typically focus on working within that established framework. We don't tend to look at a schedule and then demand that the railway company route a train to a different location at a different time; in most cases it's easier to fit into the system than to buck it. But that keeps us from asking important questions: Should this train be on another schedule? Should these tracks be ripped up and laid elsewhere? Or, maybe, should we not be riding trains at all in favor of some other transportation system?

Any claim to neutrality is illusory; there is no neutral ground on which to stand anywhere in the world. Rather than fret about that, we should embrace it and acknowledge that open discussion of the politics of knowledge claims is essential to a healthy intellectual and political culture. Everyone, no matter what their political position, should have to articulate and defend the values and assumptions on which their claims are made. The other option is intellectual stagnation and political decline, which describes the state of contemporary journalism.

Chapter 8:
Journalism: Royal, Prophetic, Apocalyptic

Intellectuals in every field have choices about how to define their mission, which will affect how they position themselves in relationship to power and privilege. To explore those choices, I want to focus on one specific type of intellectual work, journalism, though these observations are relevant more generally. Journalism is a good place to look more closely because it is the intellectual arena where illusions of neutrality are most institutionalized, and because in a mass-mediated world it is a crucial institution in the shaping of public perceptions about almost everything.

The first task is to define journalism. Ideally, journalists offer the public, in a timely fashion, a critical, independent source of information, analysis, and the varied opinions needed by citizens who want to play a meaningful role in the formation of public policy. The key terms are "critical" and "independent"—to fulfill the promise of a free press, journalists must be willing to critique not only specific people and policies, but the systems out of which they emerge, and they must be as free as possible from constraining influences, both overt and subtle. Included in that definition is an understanding of democracy—"a meaningful role in the formation of public policy"—as more than just lining up to vote in elections that offer competing sets of elites who represent roughly similar programs.

This discussion will focus on what is typically called mainstream journalism, the corporate-commercial news media. These are the journalists who work for daily newspapers, broadcast and cable television, and the rapidly expanding platforms on the internet and other digital devices. Although there are many types of independent and alternative journalism of varying quality, the vast majority of Americans receive the vast majority of their news from these mainstream sources, which are almost always organized as large corporations and funded primarily by advertising.

Right-wing politicians and commentators sometimes refer to the mainstream media as the "lamestream," implying that journalists are comically incompetent and incapable of providing an accurate account of the world, likely due to a lack of understanding of conservatives. While many elite journalists may be dismissive of the cultural values of conservatives, this critique from the right ignores the key questions about journalism's relationship to power. Focusing on the cultural politics of individual reporters and editors—pointing out that they tend to be less religious and more supportive of gay and women's rights than the general public, for example—diverts attention from more crucial questions about how the institutional politics of corporate owners and managers shapes the news and keeps mainstream journalism safely within a centrist/right conventional wisdom.

The managers of commercial news organizations in the United States typically reject that claim by citing the unbreachable "firewall" between the journalistic and the business sides of the operation, which is supposed to allow journalists to pursue any story without interference from the corporate front office. This exchange I had with a newspaper editor captures the ideology: After listening to my summary of this critique of the commercial news media system in the United States, this editor (let's call him Joe) told me proudly: "No one from corporate headquarters has ever called me to tell me what to run in my paper." I asked Joe if it were possible that he simply had internalized the value system of the folks who run the corporation (and, by extension, the folks who run the world), and therefore they never needed to give him direct instructions. He rejected that, reasserting his independence from any force outside his newsroom.

I countered: "Let's say, for the purposes of discussion, that you and I were equally capable journalists in terms of professional skills, that we were both reasonable candidates for the job of editor-in-chief that you hold. If we had both applied for the job, do you think your corporate bosses would have ever considered me for the position, given my politics? Would I, for even a second, have been seen by them to be a viable candidate for the job?"

Joe's politics are pretty conventional, well within the range of mainstream Republicans and Democrats—he supports big business and U.S. supremacy in global politics and economics. In other words, he's a capitalist and imperialist. On some political issues, Joe and I would agree, but we diverge sharply on the core questions of the nature of the economy and foreign policy.

Joe pondered my question and conceded that I was right, that his bosses would never hire someone with my politics, no matter how qualified, to run one of their newspapers. The conversation trailed off, and we parted without resolving our differences. I would like to think my critique at least got Joe to question his platitudes, but I never saw any evidence of that. In his subsequent writing and public comments that I read and heard, Joe continued to assert that a news media system dominated by for-profit corporations was the best way to produce the critical, independent journalism that citizens in a democracy needed. Because he was in a position of some privilege and status, nothing compelled Joe to respond to my challenge.

Partly as a result of many such conversations, I continue to search for new ways to present a critique of mainstream journalism that might break through that ideological wall. Here I will try theological terms, invoking the royal, prophetic, and apocalyptic traditions. Though journalism is a secular institution, the struggles of intellectuals with power is also a part of religious traditions, which provides a helpful vocabulary. The use of these terms is not meant to imply support for any particular religious tradition, or for religion more generally, but only recognizes that the fundamental struggles of human history play out in religious and secular settings, and we can learn from all of that history.

Royal Journalism

Most of today's mainstream corporate-commercial journalism is royal journalism, using the term "royal" not to describe a specific form of executive power but as a critique of a system that concentrates authority and marginalizes the needs of ordinary people. The royal tradition, in this context, describes ancient Israel, the Roman empire, European monarchs, or contemporary America—societies in which those holding concentrated wealth and power can ignore the needs of the bulk of the population, societies where the wealthy and powerful offer pious platitudes about their beneficence as they pursue policies to enrich themselves.

Theologian Walter Brueggemann identifies this royal consciousness in ancient Israel after it sank into disarray, when Solomon overturned Moses—affluence, oppressive social policy, and static religion replaced a God of liberation with one used to serve an empire. This dangerous royal consciousness develops not only in top leaders but throughout the privileged sectors, often filtering down to a wider public that accepts royal power. Brueggemann labels this a false consciousness: "The royal consciousness leads people to numbness, especially to numbness about death."[66]

---

66 Walter Brueggemann, *The Prophetic Imagination*, 2nd ed. (Minneapolis: Fortress Press, 2001), p. 41.

The inclusion of the United States in a list of royalist societies may seem odd, given the democratic traditions of the country, but consider a nation that has been at war for more than a decade, in which economic inequality and the resulting suffering has dramatically deepened for the past four decades, in which the level of climate change denial has increased as the evidence of the threat becomes undeniable. Brueggemann describes such a culture as one that is "competent to implement almost anything and to imagine almost nothing."[67]

Almost all mainstream corporate-commercial journalism is, in this sense, royal journalism. It is journalism without the imagination needed to move outside the framework created by existing systems of power. CNN, MSNBC, and FOX News all practice royal journalism. *The New York Times* is ground zero for royal journalism. Marking these institutions as royalist doesn't mean no good journalism ever emerges from them, or that they employ no journalists who are capable of challenging the royal arrangements. Instead, the term recognizes that these institutions lack the imagination necessary to step outside of the royal consciousness on a regular basis. Over time, they add to the numbness rather than jolt people out of it.

The royal consciousness of our day is defined by unchallengeable commitments to an industrial worldview, within a hierarchical economy, run by an imperial nation-state. These technological, economic, and national fundamentalisms produce a certain kind of story about ourselves, a dominant narrative that Brueggemann describes as "therapeutic, technological, consumerist militarism." The dominant culture encourages the belief that we can have anything we want without obligations to anyone within a system that fosters "competitive productivity, motivated by pervasive anxiety about having enough, or being enough, or being in control." All of this bolsters notions of "US exceptionalism that gives warrant to the usurpatious pursuit of commodities in the name of freedom, at the expense of the neighbor."[68]

If one believes royal arrangements are just and sustainable, then royal journalism could be defended. If the royal tradition requires deep critique, than a different journalism is necessary.

---

67 Ibid., p. 40.
68 Walter Brueggemann, *The Practice of Prophetic Imagination* (Minneapolis: Fortress Press, 2012), p. 4.

Prophetic Journalism

Given the failure of existing systems and the multiple crises those systems have generated, the ideals of journalism call for a prophetic journalism.[69] The first step in defending that claim is to remember what real prophets are not: They are not people who predict the future or demand that others follow them in lockstep. In the Hebrew Bible and Christian tradition, prophets are the figures who remind the people of the best of the tradition and point out how the people have strayed. In those traditions, using our prophetic imagination and speaking in a prophetic voice requires no special status in society, and no sense of being special. Claiming the prophetic tradition requires only honesty and courage.

When we strip away supernatural claims and delusions of grandeur, we can understand the prophetic as the calling out of injustice, the willingness not only to confront the abuses of the powerful but to acknowledge our own complicity. To speak prophetically requires us first to see honestly—both how our world is structured by systems that create unjust and unsustainable conditions, and how we who live in the privileged parts of the world are implicated in those systems. To speak prophetically is to refuse to shrink from what we discover or from our own place in these systems. We must confront the powers that be, and ourselves.

The Hebrew Bible offers us many models. Amos and Hosea, Jeremiah and Isaiah—all rejected the pursuit of wealth or power and argued for the centrality of kindness and justice. The prophets condemned corrupt leaders but also called out all those privileged people in society who had turned from the demands of justice, which the faith makes central to human life. In his analysis of these prophets, the scholar and activist Rabbi Abraham Joshua Heschel concluded:

> Above all, the prophets remind us of the moral state of a people: Few are guilty, but all are responsible. If we admit

---

69 I use this term to describe an ideal that all journalists should aspire to achieve. One former journalist and journalism professor uses the term in a slightly different and more limited way, to describe a segment of the existing industry. He defines "prophetic journalism" as "a journalism of passion, polemic, and moral opinion that has come to exist alongside the modern ethic of objectivity and the commercial elements of profit making that dictate so much of what journalism constitutes today." Doug Underwood, *From Yahweh to Yahoo! The Religious Roots of the Secular Press* (Urbana: University of Illinois Press, 2002), p. 21.

that the individual is in some measure conditioned or affected by the spirit of society, an individual's crime discloses society's corruption. In a community not indifferent to suffering, uncompromisingly impatient with cruelty and falsehood, continually concerned for God and every man, crime would be infrequent rather than common.[70]

Following Brueggemann's critique of royal consciousness, the task of those speaking prophetically is to "penetrate the numbness in order to face the body of death in which we are caught" and "penetrate despair so that new futures can be believed in and embraced by us."[71]

Brueggemann encourages preachers to think of themselves as "handler[s] of the prophetic tradition," a job description that also applies to other intellectual professions, including journalism. Brueggemann argues that this isn't about intellectuals imposing their views and values on others, but about being willing to "connect the dots":

> Prophetic preaching does not put people in crisis. Rather it names and makes palpable the crisis already pulsing among us. When the dots are connected, it will require naming the defining sins among us of environmental abuse, neighborly disregard, long-term racism, self-indulgent consumerism, all the staples from those ancient truthtellers translated into our time and place.[72]

None of this requires journalists to advocate for specific politicians, parties, or political programs; we don't need journalists to become propagandists. Journalists should strive for real independence, but not confuse that with an illusory neutrality that mainstream journalists invoke to stay safely within the boundaries defined by the powerful. Again, real independence means the ability to critique not just the worst abuses by the powerful within the systems, but to critique the systems themselves.

---

70 Abraham J. Heschel, *The Prophets* (New York: HarperCollins, 1962/2001), p. 19.
71 Brueggemann, *The Prophetic Imagination*, p. 117.
72 Brueggemann, *The Practice of Prophetic Imagination*, p. 69.

Apocalyptic Journalism

Invoking the prophetic in the face of royal consciousness does not promise quick change and a carefree future, but it implies that a disastrous course can be corrected. But what if the justification for such hope evaporates? When prophetic warnings have not been heeded, what comes next? This is the time when an apocalyptic sensibility is needed.

Again, to be clear: "Apocalypse" in this context does not mean lakes of fire, rivers of blood, or bodies lifted up. The shift from the prophetic to the apocalyptic can instead mark the point when hope in existing systems is no longer possible and we must think in dramatically new ways. Invoking the apocalyptic recognizes the end of something. It's not about rapture but a rupture severe enough to change the nature of the whole game.

So, while the prophetic imagination helps us analyze and strategize about the historical moment we're in, it is based on a faith that the systems in which we live can be reshaped to stop the worst consequences of the royal consciousness, to shake off that numbness of death in time. What if that is no longer possible? Then it is time to think about what's on the other side. Because no one can predict the future, these two approaches are not mutually exclusive; people should not be afraid to think prophetically and apocalyptically at the same time. We can simultaneously explore immediate changes in the existing systems and think about new systems.

Fred Guterl, the executive editor of *Scientific American*, models that spirit when he describes himself on the "techno-optimistic side of the spectrum" but does not shy away from a blunt discussion of the challenges humans face:

> There's no going back on our reliance on computers and high-tech medicine, agriculture, power generation, and so forth without causing vast human suffering—unless you want to contemplate reducing the world population by many billions of people. We have climbed out on a technological limb, and turning back is a disturbing option. We are dependent on our technology, yet our technology now presents the seeds of our own destruction. It's a dilemma. I

don't pretend to have a way out. We should start by being aware of the problem.[73]

I don't share Guterl's techno-optimism, but it strikes me as different from the technological fundamentalism critiqued earlier. He doesn't deny the magnitude of the problems and recognizes the real possibility, perhaps even the inevitability, of massive social dislocation. Though he ends up with a different sense of where hope lies, he doesn't avoid reality:

> [W]e're going to need the spirit with which these ideas were hatched to solve the problems we have created. Tossing aside technological optimism is not a realistic option. This doesn't mean technology is going to save us. We may still be doomed. But without it, we are surely doomed.[74]

A bit closer to my own assessment is James Lovelock, a Fellow of the Royal Society whose work led to the detection of the widespread presence CFCs in the atmosphere. Most famous for his "Gaia hypothesis" that understands both the living and nonliving parts of the earth as a complex system that can be thought of as a single organism, he suggests that we face these stark realities immediately:

> The great party of the twentieth century is coming to an end, and unless we now start preparing our survival kit we will soon be just another species eking out an existence in the few remaining habitable regions. … We should be the heart and mind of the Earth, not its malady. So let us be brave and cease thinking of human needs and rights alone and see that we have harmed the living Earth and need to make our peace with Gaia.[75]

In a culture that encourages, even demands, optimism no matter what the facts, it is important to consider alternative endings. As Barbara Ehrenreich points out, this obsession with so-called posi-

---

73 Guterl, *The Fate of the Species*, p. 5.
74 Ibid., p. 170.
75 James Lovelock, *The Revenge of Gaia: Earth's Climate Crisis and the Fate of Humanity* (New York: Basic, 2006), p. xiv.

tive thinking undermines critical thinking and produces anxiety of its own.[76] Anything that blocks us from looking honestly at reality, no matter how harsh the reality, must be rejected. To borrow from James Baldwin, "Not everything that is faced can be changed; but nothing can be changed until it is faced." That line is from an essay titled "As Much Truth as One Can Bear,"[77] about the struggles of artists to help a society, such as white-supremacist America, face the depth of its pathology. Baldwin, writing with a focus on relationships between humans, suggested that a great writer attempts "to tell as much of the truth as one can bear, and then a little more." If we think of Baldwin as sounding a prophetic call, an apocalyptic invocation would be "to tell as much of the truth as one can bear, and then all the rest of the truth, whether we can bear it or not."

That task is difficult enough when people are relatively free to pursue the truth without constraints. Are the dominant corporate-commercial/advertising-supported media outlets likely to encourage journalists to pursue the projects that might lead to such questions? If not, the apocalyptic journalism we need is more likely to emerge from the margins, where people are not trapped by illusions of neutrality or concerned about professional status.

The apocalyptic tradition reminds us that the absence of hope does not have to leave us completely hopeless, that life is always at the same time about death, and then rejuvenation. While all the other creatures of this world will experience death, we will not only experience death but have to ponder it. When the evidence of our failure is final and all hope is gone, can we retain our ability to imagine beyond the failure? Earth is over, but we can start to imagine what we can salvage on Eaarth.

---

76 Barbara Ehrenreich, *Bright-sided: How Positive Thinking Is Undermining America* (New York: Picador, 2010).
77 James Baldwin, "As Much Truth As One Can Bear," in Randall Kenan, ed., *The Cross of Redemption: Uncollected Writings* (New York: Pantheon, 2010), pp. 28–34.

Conclusion: Future Hope?

Here's my experience in speaking apocalyptically: No matter how carefully I craft a statement of concern about the future of humans, no matter how often I deny a claim to special gifts of prognostication, no matter now clearly I reject supernatural explanations or solutions, I can be certain that a significant component of any audience will refuse to take me seriously. Some of those people will make a joke about "Mr. Doom and Gloom." Others will suggest that such talk is no different than conspiracy theorists' ramblings about how international bankers, secret cells of communists, or crypto-fascists are using the United Nations to create a one-world government. Even the most measured and careful talk of the coming dramatic change in the place of humans on Earth leads to accusations that one is unnecessarily alarmist, probably paranoid, certainly irrelevant to serious discussion about social and ecological issues. In the United States, talk of the future is expected to be upbeat, predicting expansion and progress, or at least maintenance of our "way of life."

Apocalyptic thinking allows us to let go of those fanciful visions of the future. As singer/songwriter John Gorka puts it: "The old future's gone/We can't get to there from here."[78] The comfortable futures that we are comfortable imagining are no longer available to us because of the reckless way we've been rolling the dice; there is nothing to save us from ourselves. Our task is to deal with our future on Eaarth, without delusions of deliverance, either divine or technological. This planet is not a way station in a journey to some better place; it is our home, the only home we will know. We will make our peace with ourselves, each other, and the larger living world here.

The first step in thinking sensibly about the future, of course, is reviewing the past. The uncertainty of our future will be easier to accept and the strength to persevere will be easier to summon if we recognize:

—We are animals. For all our considerable rational capacities, we are driven by non-rational forces that cannot be fully understood or completely controlled. Even the most careful scientist is largely an emotional creature, just like everyone else.
—We are band/tribal animals. Whatever kind of political unit we live in today, our evolutionary history is in small groups; that's how we are designed to live.

---

78 John Gorka, "Old Future" from the CD "Old Futures Gone," Red House Records, 2003.

—We are band/tribal animals living in a global world. The consequences of the past 10,000 years of human history have left us dealing with human problems on a global scale, and with 7 billion people on the planet, there's no point in fantasizing about a retreat to Eden.

With that history in mind, we should go easy on ourselves. As Wes Jackson said, we are a species out of context, facing the unique task of being the first animals who will have to self-consciously impose limits on ourselves if we are to survive, reckoning not just with what we do in our specific place on the planet but with what other people are doing around the world. This is no small task, and we are bound to fail often. We may never stop failing, and that is possibly the most daunting challenge we must face: Can we persevere in the quest for justice and sustainability even if we had good reasons to believe that both projects ultimately will fail? Can we live with that possibility? Can we ponder that and yet still commit ourselves to loving action toward others and the non-human world?

Said differently: What if our species is an evolutionary dead end? What if those adaptations that produced our incredible evolutionary success—our ability to understand certain aspects of how the world works and manipulate that world to our short-term advantage—are the very qualities that guarantee our human systems will degrade the life-sustaining systems of the world? What if that which has allowed us to dominate will be that which destroys us? What if humanity's story is a dramatic tragedy in the classical sense, a tale in which the seeds of the hero's destruction are to be found within, and history is the unfolding of the inevitable fall?

We love stories of individual heroes, and collectively we tend to think of ourselves as the heroic species. The question we might ask, uncomfortably, about those tales of heroism: Is *Homo sapiens* an epic hero or a tragic one? Literature scholars argue over the specific definitions of the terms "epic" and "tragedy," but in common usage an epic celebrates the deeds of a hero who is favored by, and perhaps descended from, the gods. These heroes overcome adversity to do great things in the service of great causes. Epic heroes win.

A tragic hero loses, but typically not because of an external force. The essence of tragedy is what Aristotle called "hamartia," an error in judgment made because of some character flaw, such as hubris. That excessive pride of protagonists becomes their downfall. Although some traditions talk about the sin of pride, most of us understand that taking some pride in ourselves is psychologically healthy. The problem is excessive pride, when we elevate ourselves and lose a sense of the equal value of others. When we fall into hubris individually, the consequences can be disastrous for us and those around us. When we fall into that hubris as a species—when we ignore the consequences of the exploitation on which our "life-style" is based—the consequences are more dramatic.

What if our task is to give up the dream of the human species as special? And what if the global forces set in motion during the high-energy/high-technology era are beyond the point of no return? Surrounded by the big majestic buildings and tiny sophisticated electronic gadgets created through human cleverness, it's easy for us to believe we are smart enough to run a complex world. But cleverness is not wisdom, and the ability to create does not guarantee we can control the destruction we have unleashed. It may be that there is no way to rewrite this larger epic, that too much of the tragedy has already been played out.

But here's the good news: While tragic heroes meet an unhappy fate, a community can learn from the protagonist's fall. Even tragic heroes can, at the end, celebrate the dignity of the human spirit in their failure. That may be our task, to recognize that we can't reverse course in time to prevent our ultimate failure, but that in the time remaining we can recognize our hamartia, name our hubris, and do what we can to undo the damage.

That may be the one chance for us to be truly heroic, by learning to leave center stage gracefully, to stop trying to run the world and to accept a place in the world. We have to take our lives seriously but take Life more seriously.

Undertaking that, honestly, would be both dangerous and joyful. In his meditation on the role of writers, Baldwin offered a challenge that can be applied to intellectuals more generally, and in some sense to everyone:

> We are the generation that must throw everything into the endeavor to remake America into what we say we want it to be. Without this endeavor, we will perish. However immoral or subversive this may sound to some, it is the writer who must always remember that morality, if it is to

remain or become morality, must be perpetually examined, cracked, changed, made new. He must remember, however powerful the many who would rather forget, that life is the only touchstone and that life is dangerous, and that without the joyful acceptance of this danger, there can never be any safety for anyone, ever, anywhere.[79]

"A joyful acceptance of danger" would make a great motto for intellectuals today. We certainly live in a dangerous time, if we take seriously the data that our vast intellectual enterprises have produced. Ironically, the majority of intellectuals who are part of those enterprises prefer to ignore the implications of that data. The reasons for that will of course vary, and there is no reason to pretend these issues are simple or that we can line up intellectuals in simple categories of good/bad, brave/cowardly, honest/dishonest. Reasonable people can agree on the data and disagree on interpretation and analysis. Again, my argument is not that anyone who does not share my interpretation and analysis is obviously wrong or corrupt; many of the assertions I have made require more lengthy argument than available in this space.

But I hold to one point without equivocation: When the privileged intellectuals subsidized by the institutions of the dominant culture look away from the difficult issues that we face today, they are failing to meet their moral obligations. The more privileged the intellectual, the greater the responsibility to use our resources, status, and autonomy to face these issues. There is a lot riding on whether we have the courage and the strength to accept that danger, joyfully. This harsh assessment, and the grief that must accompany it, is not a rejection of joy. The two, grief and joy, are not mutually exclusive but, in fact, rely on each other, and define the human condition. As Wendell Berry puts it, we live on "the human estate of grief and joy."[80]

This inevitably leads to the question: where can we find hope? My short answer: Don't ask someone else where to find it. Create it through your actions. Hope is not something we find, but is something we earn. No one has the right to be hopeful until they expend energy to make hope possible. Gorka's song expresses this: "The old future's dead and gone/Never to return/There's a new way through

---

79 Baldwin, "As Much Truth As One Can Bear," p. 34.
80 Berry, *The Unsettling of America*, p. 106.

the hills ahead/This one we'll have to earn/This one we'll have to earn."

Berry speaks repeatedly of the importance of daily practice, of building a better world in a practical ways that nurture real bonds in real communities that know their place in the world. He applies this same idea to a discussion of hope:

> [Y]ou're not under any obligation to construct a hope for the whole human race. What you are required to do is to be intelligent. And that means you've got to have an array of examples you want more or less to understand. Some are not perfect, and others are awful, and to be intelligent you've got to know why some are better than the others.[81]

If people demand that intellectuals provide hope—or, worse, if intellectuals believe it is their job to give people hope—then offering platitudes about hope is just another way of avoiding the difficult questions. Clamoring for hope can be a dangerous diversion. But if the discussion of hope leads to action, even in the face of situations that may be hopeless, then we can hold onto what Albert Camus called a "stubborn hope":

> Tomorrow the world may burst into fragments. In that threat hanging over our heads there is a lesson of truth. As we face such s a future, hierarchies, titles, honors are reduced to what they are in reality: a passing puff of smoke. And the only certainty left to us is that of naked suffering, common to all, intermingling its roots with those of a stubborn hope.[82]

I would call this a hope beyond hope, the willingness not only to embrace that danger but to find joy in it. The systems that structure our world have done more damage than we can understand, but no matter how dark the world grows, there is a light within. That is the message of the best of our theological and secular philosophical traditions, a recurring theme of the best of our art. Wendell Berry has been returning to this theme for decades in essays, fiction, and

---

81 Joshua J. Yates, "A Conversation with Wendell Berry and Wes Jackson," *Hedgehog Review*, Summer 2012, p. 71.
82 Albert Camus, "The Wager of Our Generation," in *Resistance, Rebellion, and Death* (New York: Vintage, 1960), pp. 239–240.

poetry, and it is the subject of one of his Sabbath poems[83]:

> It is hard to have hope. It is harder as you grow old,
> for hope must not depend on feeling good
> and there is the dream of loneliness at absolute midnight.
> You also have withdrawn belief in the present reality
> of the future, which surely will surprise us,
> and hope is harder when it cannot come by prediction
> any more than by wishing. But stop dithering.
> The young ask the old to hope. What will you tell them?
> Tell them at least what you say to yourself.

This is what I say to myself: Whatever our chances of surviving, we define ourselves in the present moment by what we do. There are two basic tasks in front of us. First, we should commit some of our energy to movements that focus on the question of justice in this world, especially those of us with the privilege that is rooted in that injustice. As a middle-class American white man, I can see plenty of places to continue working, in movements dedicated to ending white supremacy, patriarchy, capitalism, and U.S. wars of domination.

I also think there is important work to be done in experiments to prepare for what will come in this new future that we can't yet describe in detail. Whatever the limits of our predictive capacity, we can be pretty sure we will need ways of organizing ourselves to help us live in a world with less energy and fewer material goods. We all have to develop the skills needed for that world (such as farming and gardening with fewer inputs, food preparation and storage, and basic tinkering), and we will need to recover a deep sense of community that has disappeared from many of our lives. This means abandoning a sense of ourselves as consumption machines, which the contemporary culture promotes, and deepening our notions of what it means to be humans in search of meaning. We have to learn to tell different stories about our sense of self, our connection to others, and our place in nature. The stories we tell will matter, as will the skills we learn.

Berry's basis for hope begins with a recognition of where we are and who we are, at our best:

---

83 Wendell Berry, "Sabbaths 2007, VI," in *Leavings: Poems* (Berkeley, CA: Counterpoint, 2010), p. 91–93.

Found your hope, then, on the ground under your feet.
Your hope of Heaven, let it rest on the ground
underfoot. Be lighted by the light that falls
freely upon it after the darkness of the nights
and the darkness of our ignorance and madness.
Let it be lighted also by the light that is within you,
which is the light of imagination. By it you see
the likeness of people in other places to yourself
in your place. It lights invariably the need for care
toward other people, other creatures, in other places
as you would ask them for care toward your place and you.

In my own life, I continue to work on those questions of justice in existing movements, but I have shifted a considerable amount of time to helping build local networks that can create a place for those experiments. Different people will move toward different efforts depending on talents and temperaments; we should all follow our hearts and minds to apply ourselves where it makes sense, given who we are and where we live. After offering several warnings about arrogance, I'm not about to suggest I know best what work other people should do. If there is any reason for hope, it will be in direct proportion to our capacity for humility and seeing ourselves as part of, not on top of, the larger living world. Berry ends that Sabbath poem not with false optimism but a blunt reminder of how easy it is for us to fall out of right relation with ourselves, others, and the larger living world:

No place at last is better than the world. The world
is no better than its places. Its places at last
are no better than their people while their people
continue in them. When the people make
dark the light within them, the world darkens.

The argument I have made rests on an unsentimental assessment of the physical world and the life-threatening consequences of human activity over the past 10,000 years. We would be wise not to plan on supernatural forces or human inventions to save us from ourselves. It is unlikely that we will be delivered to a promised land by divine or technological intervention. Wishing the world were less harsh will not magically make it less harsh. We should not give into the temptation to believe in magic. As James Howard Kunstler puts it, we should stop "clamoring desperately for rescue remedies that would allow them to continue living exactly the way they were used to living, with all the accustomed comforts."[84]

But we should keep telling stories. Our stories do not change the physical world, but they have the potential to change us. In that sense, the poet Muriel Rukeyser was right when she said, "The universe is made of stories, not of atoms."[85]

Whatever particular work intellectuals do, they are also storytellers. Artists tell stories, but so do scientists and engineers, teachers and preachers. Our work is always both embedded in a story and advancing a story. Intellectual work matters not just for what it discovers about how the world works, but for what story it tells about those discoveries.

To think apocalyptically is not to give up on ourselves, but only to give up on the arrogant stories we modern humans have been telling about ourselves. Our hope for a decent future—indeed, any hope for even the idea of a future—depends on our ability to tell stories not of how humans have ruled the world but how we can live in the world. The royal must give way to the prophetic and the apocalyptic. The central story of power—that the domination/subordination dynamic is natural and inevitable—must give way to stories of dignity, solidarity, equality. We must resist not only the cruelty of repression but the seduction of comfort.

The songs we sing matter at least as much as the machines we build. Power always assumes it can control. Our task is to resist that control. Gorka offers that reminder, of the latent power of our stories, in the fancifully titled song "Flying Red Horse":

> They think they can tame you, name you and frame you,
> Aim you where you don't belong.
> They know where you've been but not where you're going,
> And that is the source of the songs.[86]

---

84 Kunstler, *Too Much Magic*, p. 7.
85 Muriel Rukeyser, "The Speed of Darkness," in *The Speed of Darkness* (New York: Random House, 1968), stanza 9, lines 3–4.
86 John Gorka, "Flying Red Horse" from the CD "Out of the Valley," Red House Records, 1994.